BATTLEFIELD
WALKS
SCOTLAND

D0756256

BATTLEFIELD WALKS SCOTLAND

David Clark

SUTTON PUBLISHING

First published in 1996 by
Sutton Publishing Limited · Phoenix Mill
Thrupp · Stroud · Gloucestershire · GL5 2BU

British Library Cataloguing in Publication Data

A catalogue record for this book is available from the British Library

ISBN 0 7509 0261 2

 ^{TM} ALAN SUTTON™ and SUTTON™ are the
trade marks of Sutton Publishing Limited

Typeset in 10/12 pt Plantin Light.
Typesetting and origination by
Sutton Publishing Limited.
Printed in Great Britain by
WBC Limited, Bridgend.

CONTENTS

Battle sites: General map

INTRODUCTION

The arguments for fostering an interest in the exploration of battlefields are encapsulated in Peter Marren's introduction to his *Grampian Battlefields*, and specifically in his reminder that the only monument to the battle of Alford, scene of one of Montrose's famous victories in which 2,000 Scots died, lies buried beneath a rubbish dump. Such is the interest in battlefields, and in Scottish battlefields in particular, that Marren's superb book, written in 1980, remained unpublished for ten years.

To an extent, public perception is undergoing a change, for there is currently a temporary revival of interest in Scottish battlefields. The success of the Mel Gibson movie *Braveheart* has resulted in the appearance of several lavishly illustrated publications on a battlefield theme. When the current craze subsides, however, as it surely will, the film producers will look for alternative money-spinners, the publishing houses will turn their attention to other themes, the crowds will go home – and the Alford monument will still lie buried beneath a rubbish dump.

It becomes important, therefore, that efforts should be made to encourage a lasting interest in battlefields, which are as much a part of our heritage as castles and stately homes. The compilation of a national *Battlefields Register* has done much to raise such an awareness in England, whereas Scottish battlefields remain a largely unprotected species, the likely prey of rapacious builders of housing developments, industrial estates and dual carriageways.

Interest may be stimulated in a number of ways. For example, battlefield exploration may be incorporated into the school curriculum – directly in the study of history and indirectly as a nominated topic within other subject areas, such as geography. Ultimately, however, awareness raising exercises are insufficient for, as far as battlefield survival is concerned, there is no substitute for site exploration. Rights of way across battlefields must be kept open and, despite the obligations of local authorities to maintain access, many ancient paths have fallen into disuse. In this respect, rambling clubs could do much to help by including the occasional organized battlefield walk in their quarterly programmes. More often than not, it is left to the individual to keep the door to the past open.

With over two dozen identifiable battles having occurred in north-east Scotland alone, the choice of sites for inclusion in this book was always going to be difficult. However, some important battlefields, such as Justice

INTRODUCTION

Mills, Aberdeen (1644) have been obliterated as a result of urban development, while the actual location of earlier sites, such as Mons Graupius (AD 84) is in doubt, thus narrowing the range of possibilities. In the end, the sites were selected, in part for their historical significance, for their accessibility, and because they constitute attractive walks in their own right.

The chapters are divided into well-defined sections, giving background information, descriptions of the campaigns and battles, and of the results. Suggested routes for on-site explorations of the battlefields are supported with hints for additional explorations of wider areas and further information concerning accessibility. To gain the most from a site visit, it is important to engage in a little research beforehand. In this respect, references should be followed up and contacts made, as recommended. Undoubtedly, the most satisfying form of learning is that of self-discovery, and conscientious explorers will be pleasantly surprised at encountering, without too much effort, the occasional battlefield feature not mentioned in the text.

As far as practical considerations are concerned, it will be seen that the selected sites fall very roughly into three geographical groups: East Lothian (Dunbar, East Fortune, Pinkie Heugh and Prestonpans); Central (Bannockburn, Kilsyth, Falkirk, Sheriffmuir and Drumclog); Highland (Killiecrankie, Auldearn and Culloden). Thus, it is possible to confine one's attention to a specific grouping. Alternatively, one may wish to visit all twelve – an objective which can be accomplished (by car) within one week. However, a two-week tour is ideal, with a day – and time to spare – to devote to each site and its environs. The best time of year to visit is undoubtedly the summer months, to allow for admission to battlefield visitor centres, museums etc., some of which enjoy rather short seasons.

For most of the walks, stout shoes will suffice, although the purchase of a pair of walking boots will pay dividends in terms of reducing wear and tear on one's feet. Boots are recommended for Kilsyth, Sheriffmuir and Killiecrankie. Additional kit may include a light shoulder bag, containing necessary liquid refreshment and an umbrella – possibly attracting the ridicule of seasoned ramblers, but essential for avoiding the discomfort of continuing a walk when soaked to the skin in the early stages. Although the sketch maps should prove adequate guides, the relevant Ordnance Survey Pathfinder map for each area (or alternative street plans, where recommended) will prove invaluable.

Most experienced ramblers will be aware of the basic difference between the Ordnance Survey Pathfinder maps of England and those of Scotland. Whereas the former have public rights of way clearly marked, the latter do not. In the past, this has presented no problem, for in Scotland there has always been a widespread tradition of freedom to roam. Today, many properties are being bought by the English, for whom home is not home without the extraneous additions of barbed wire fences and 'Keep Out' signs. However, the author experienced no difficulties during his explorations of the sites discussed. In this respect, the reader will benefit from his mistakes – whether it be the avoidance of blundering onto private land, sinking into bogs or simply getting lost.

THE BATTLE OF BANNOCKBURN
23–4 June 1314

Introduction

When, in March 1286, the King of Scotland, Alexander III, tumbled from his horse to his death, he also plunged his country into turmoil. At first, it appeared that order might prevail, for there was general agreement among the Scottish magnates that Alexander should be succeeded by his granddaughter, Margaret of Norway. There was even talk of a possible marriage between the infant princess and Prince Edward, son of Edward I of England, with a view to bringing to an end centuries of enmity between the two kingdoms. Unfortunately, Margaret died en route to Scotland, thus opening up the field to the claims of rival candidates.

Foremost among the contenders were John Balliol and the octogenarian Earl of Annandale. Both claimants had strong support and once again, civil war seemed inevitable. In instances of a disputed succession, it was not unusual in medieval Europe for the opposing factions to turn to independent arbitration. Thus, in June 1291, Edward I found himself in the enviable position of being asked to reach a decision on the matter. Skilfully, the English king manipulated the situation to his advantage, with the Scots being compelled to pledge their fealty to him. Having established this principle, Edward proceeded to make a choice. The king of Scotland, he decided, would be John Balliol. In legal terms, Balliol was probably marginally ahead, besides which Edward thought he would pose less of a threat to the security of England than the warlike Annandale.

Balliol proved to be a weak king, amenable to English influence and, as a result, unpopular with his subjects. When, in 1294, England declared war on France, the Scots were quick to seize the opportunity of siding with King Philip and the following year, the Scottish Parliament – on its own authority – concluded a treaty with the French. Edward responded by mounting an invasion of Scotland. Intent on teaching the Scots a lesson they would never forget, he led an English army in an onslaught on Berwick, for many years an important centre of commerce. Quickly overrunning the flimsy defences, the invaders embarked upon an orgy of slaughter which lasted for two days. When, at last, Edward called a halt, the dead were piled high in the streets.

Word of the atrocities committed at Berwick travelled fast, and save for a half-hearted stand at Dunbar on 27 April 1296, when an army of Scottish nobles were soundly beaten by the Earl of Surrey (see p. 63), there was little further opposition. The hapless Balliol was consigned to the Tower of London and the dormant Annandale claim to the throne brushed aside as Edward took possession of Scotland for himself. Berwick became his administrative capital, Scottish castles were garrisoned by English troops, and the Stone of Scone, symbol of Scottish sovereignty, removed to Westminster Abbey.

No sooner had Edward departed than there began to develop pockets of resistance, which gradually blossomed into organized revolt under the guidance of a Scottish knight, William Wallace. A gifted general, Wallace, at the head of a rapidly growing army, was soon creating havoc on a scale which Edward could not afford to ignore, and on 11 September 1297, the Earl of Surrey closed with him at Stirling Bridge. Wallace easily outmanoeuvred the ageing Surrey, veteran of the Battle of Lewes, fought more than thirty years earlier. Heavily defeated, Surrey was pursued all the way back to Berwick. Wallace's triumph was brief, for Edward, who assumed personal command of an army of 15,000 men, turned the tables on him at Falkirk on 22 July 1298. His army destroyed, Wallace escaped to France, leaving Edward, short of supplies, to turn for home, in the knowledge that his task remained unfinished, and that another would surely arise to take Wallace's place.

The Road to Bannockburn

The old Earl of Annandale (known as Robert the Competitor) had died in 1295. His son, Robert, Earl of Carrick, survived him by only nine years. For a time, Robert had served Edward I in the capacity of Governor of Carlisle thinking, perhaps, that the Annandale cause would best be served by fealty as opposed to open rebellion. Upon his death, Robert's own son – also Robert – who was then twenty-nine years of age, became head of the family. Despite the English victory at Falkirk, Edward's influence was limited to the south-east of Scotland and for a time the country had, in effect, two governments: Edward's government and a Scottish government under the direction of 'guardians' appointed, in John Balliol's enforced absence, as caretakers. Robert, who would gain lasting fame as 'Robert the Bruce', was named as a guardian. One of Robert's fellow guardians, John Comyn (The Red) entertained ambitions of his own and, following a series of quarrels with Comyn, Robert resigned from his post.

Between 1300 and 1304, Edward embarked on a number of forays over the border, but not until February 1304 did Scottish resistance collapse. Robert the Bruce, together with Robert Wishart, Bishop of Glasgow and the English magnate, Sir John Mowbray, were appointed by Edward as the new 'guardians'. At first, it seemed that Edward was recognizing the Scottish right to self-determination, but it became clear with the provisions of his subsequent 'Ordinances for the Establishment of the Land of Scotland' that he continued to view Scotland as a vassal state. With the capture and execution of Wallace, who had reappeared in Glasgow, the English triumph was complete. These were dark days for the Scots, few of whom would have been able to identify Robert the Bruce as their future saviour, perhaps failing to recognize in him the crusading zeal displayed by his grandfather.

It will never be known whether Robert's attempt to seize power was intentional, or whether it came about by accident. There is no doubt about the fact that on 10 February 1306, Robert killed John Comyn in Greyfriars Church, Dumfries. Was Comyn's death the result of yet another quarrel, or was it a carefully planned and executed assassination? Certainly, Robert lost no time in making his way to Scone, where he was crowned on 25 March 1306. Edward moved swiftly to put down this latest and most audacious insurrection, and on 18 June, the small army Robert had contrived to muster was put to flight by an English force commanded by the Earl of Pembroke. Several of Robert's most loyal supporters were captured, among them his brother, Nigel, who was summarily hanged, drawn and quartered. The Countess of Buchan, who had placed the crown upon Robert's head, was imprisoned in a wooden cage, suspended from the battlements of Berwick Castle, where she remained for four years.

Robert, whose wife and daughter had also been taken prisoner, slipped away to the Western Isles, accompanied by only a handful of faithful followers. During the winter of 1306–7, many sympathizers sought him out and soon he was able to embark upon a series of hit and run raids against the enemy. It was during this period that there occurred the legendary incident of the web-spinning spider – the creature's continuous effort encouraging him not to lose heart in his own struggle.[1] Certainly, much

1 The story goes that the downcast Robert watched a spider make six failed attempts at climbing its web, before succeeding at the seventh. This legend was popularized by Sir Walter Scott, whose skill at combining fact and fiction has led to many a misconception. According to other sources, it was Sir James Douglas who comforted Robert by recounting how he himself had witnessed a spider engaged in a similar exercise fail no less than twelve times. It may well be that no one saw a spider doing anything, but the parable does characterize the nation's qualities of tenacity and endurance.

Great Seal of Robert I, King of
Scotland (Robert the Bruce).
(British Museum)

perseverance was required, for a return to the mainland in the spring of
1307 led to the deaths of two more of his brothers while he himself narrowly
avoided capture.

Robert's fortunes took a turn for the better with a victory over the Earl of
Pembroke at Loudon Hill, an event which was followed by the timely death
of Edward I. Command of the army which the English king had been
leading into Scotland at the time of his death was taken over by the Prince of
Wales, shortly to be crowned Edward II. Where his late father would have
advanced, however, his successor retreated, giving Robert valuable time to
consolidate his position. His conquest of the kingdom he had claimed as his
own the year before took seven long years. Having secured the north and
west of Scotland, he turned his attention to the south, reducing the English
strongholds in piecemeal fashion and mounting many savage raids across
the border. Edward II, regarded generally as a perverted weakling, proved
unequal to the task of stopping the rot, and half-hearted sorties into
Scotland achieved nothing save a weakening of Edward's already waning
popularity at home. Nonetheless, Edward remained convinced that his own
salvation lay in bringing the Scots to heel, and on 17 June 1314, at Berwick,
he assembled a force of some 20,000 men to embark on a campaign
destined to culminate in one of the most comprehensive defeats ever
suffered by an English army on the field of battle.

The Battle of Bannockburn

Ostensibly, the objective of Edward's invasion was the relief of Stirling Castle, to which Edward Bruce, Robert's only surviving brother, had laid siege in 1313. Stirling's governor, Sir Philip Mowbray, had agreed to surrender the stronghold if it was not relieved by 24 June 1314. Thus, the site of the forthcoming battle would be fixed in the vicinity of Stirling, with Robert free to choose his ground.

One is almost inclined to argue that Edward's army was too large. Although the logistical problems were tackled, in part, by the provision of a supporting fleet of ships, it is said that the English baggage train was still strung out over a distance of 20 miles. If Robert, master of the art of guerilla warfare, could have spared the men, the English column surely would have been sorely pressed. Normally, the number of troops under Robert's command could be counted in hundreds rather than in thousands. Even now, in his country's hour of need, Robert could field an army of barely 10,000 men, a number which included 3,000 hastily mustered militia and only 500 cavalry. Facing them were Edward's 20,000, the precise composition of which is unknown. There may well have been in the region of 17,000 infantry, up to 1,500 heavy cavalry and perhaps 1,500 archers.

Oddly enough for a battle of such significance to both sides, the exact location of the fighting is open to debate. However, the initial defensive position selected by Robert was a wooded plateau two miles south of Stirling, known as New Park. Fronted by a river, the Bannock Burn, and surrounded by marshland, the site was rendered particularly unsuitable to cavalry attack. As it appeared likely that the English approach would be via the Edinburgh–Stirling road, the Scots dug pits on either side of it at a point below the plateau known as 'The Entry', where the landscape opened out.

On 23 June 1314, Edward's grand army, which had, indeed, taken the route predicted by Robert, halted two miles short of New Park, where it was met by Sir Philip Mowbray who had by-passed Robert's left flank by The Carse – the floodplain of the River Forth. On Mowbray's advice, Edward despatched some 300 horse under Sir Robert Clifford and Sir Henry Beaumont, to approach the castle via The Carse. However, they had progressed no further than St Ninian's Church when they were engaged by the Earl of Moray. Unable to penetrate the Scottish schiltrons,[2] Clifford and

---

2 A schiltron was a shield-troop, a dense body of spearmen protected by their shields.

Beaumont were compelled to give ground. Meanwhile, the Earls of Hereford and Gloucester, having misinterpreted Robert's deployment of his men as a sign that the Scots were about to retreat, began to move through The Entry, with a view to launching an assault on the plateau.

There now occurred the famous episode in which Hereford's nephew, Sir Henry de Bohun, who was in the van of the English column, rode forth to meet Robert in single combat. The odds appeared to be in de Bohun's favour, armed as he was with a lance, against Robert's battle-axe. In the heat of the moment, de Bohun's aim went awry and Robert shattered his skull with a single blow. Taking this as a cue to advance, the Scots put the English column to flight. As darkness fell, both sides withdrew, and so ended the first act of the English tragedy.

Although the fighting had ceased, the English army still had much to do. Only with difficulty did they manage to ford Bannock Burn, to set up camp on The Carse. Hemmed in on the low-lying marshland by Bannock Burn on their left and the Forth on their right, their only hope lay in a well-orchestrated attack, aimed at overwhelming Robert's position. For his part, Robert recognized the weak situation into which the English had unwittingly manoeuvred themselves and resolved to take the initiative himself on the following day.

At daybreak on 24 June, the Scots began descending The Carse. Their deployment took the form of four 'battles' or divisions: Edward Bruce occupied the right wing, with Sir James Douglas on the left and the Earl of Moray in the centre. Robert, commanding a fourth battle, stood to the rear while the militia, or 'wee folk' as they were known, remained on the plateau. The cavalry under Sir Robert Keith also remained uncommitted. Crammed together as they were, the English were unable to deploy effectively, standing their ground in several massed divisions, with the Earl of Gloucester leading and King Edward in the rear.

The battle was opened by the archers of both sides. Although the English archers outnumbered their Scottish counterparts, there seems to have been no effort made to use them to any tactical advantage. The first divisions to clash were those of Gloucester and Edward Bruce. Almost immediately, Gloucester was unhorsed and killed while his retainers stood and watched. Moray then brought up his own division of pikemen to come to grips with the English centre, to be followed, in turn, by Douglas on the left. Pressing home their attack, the Scots created havoc in the tightly packed English ranks, hacking their way forward with all the desperation of men who fight for their homeland.

The heavily armoured English knight was proving no match for the Scottish schiltron. Once unhorsed and unable to rise unaided, the knight would be surrounded by foot soldiers and promptly finished off. Keith's light cavalry, on the other hand, were being saved for a particular manoeuvre destined to determine the outcome of the battle. Hard pressed though the English were, Robert noted that their archers were still operating effectively on the right wing, and so he despatched Keith's horse to disperse them. This objective having been accomplished, Robert brought into play his own division, occupying the ground from which the English archers had been cleared.

The sea of bodies continued to sway back and forth, the increasing forward pressure exerted by the Scots set against the efforts of the English to break out, a stalemate broken by the intervention of the 'small folk' who, on their own initiative, came charging down the hill to join the affray. The unexpected sight of 3,000 additional Scots was enough to sow the seeds of panic among the English, many of whom in the rear never took part in the battle. At length, individuals, and then small groups within this rearguard began to slip away, the space thus created allowing the Scots to push further forward. Soon, Edward himself was at risk and his bodyguard, perceiving that the day was lost, forced him to pull back. The sight of their king in full retreat was all that was needed to break the morale of his men, while the Scots were spurred on to even greater efforts which culminated in the collapse of the English front lines.

As his army disintegrated, Edward rode for Stirling Castle, only to find that Mowbray, once more in residence, refused to admit him. Miraculously, he still evaded Robert's clutches, making his way to Dunbar, from where he took a small boat to Berwick. Much of his army was not so lucky. Many men were drowned as they tried to cross both the Forth and Bannock Burn, while those who succeeded were pursued by the rampant Scots for upwards of fifty miles. It was a famous victory for Robert who, by force of arms, had earned the right to the title: Robert I, King of Scotland.

The Aftermath

In the aftermath of a victory as comprehensive as Bannockburn, it is curious that the death count was comparatively low. Infantry dead numbered around 300 and, while estimates of slain knights vary between 200 and 700, a figure of 300 may not be too wide of the mark. The pursuit of the fleeing English was hampered by Robert's initial preoccupation with what might be happening within the walls of Stirling Castle and by the rank and file's interest in Edward's abandoned baggage train, valued at the then princely sum of £200,000. Again, wherever possible, knights were captured with a view to ransom and for use as bargaining counters in negotiations for the return of Scots held prisoner in England. Thus it is recorded that 500

Englishmen of note, who but for their potential value would have been killed, were eventually redeemed. Among the Scots who gained freedom were Robert's wife and daughter.

As underdog, Robert had proved himself a ruthless opponent, the murder of his rival, Comyn, on consecrated ground having shocked everyone. In victory, however, he could afford to exercise a measure of magnanimity, extending the hand of friendship where he might have been expected to exact a fearsome revenge. For example, the English knight, Sir Marmaduke Tweng, who had fought against Wallace at Stirling Bridge, was unhorsed at Bannockburn and threw himself on Robert's mercy. Robert greeted him as a long-lost friend, entertained him and sent him home without demanding any ransom. Similarly, many of Robert's own countrymen who had curried favour with the English, and who can have expected little in the way of clemency, were welcomed back to the fold.

Although Robert had achieved his primary objective of consolidating his position in Scotland, there remained the problem of continuing English enmity. Moves to establish amicable relations with Edward having proved unsuccessful, he countenanced a series of raids which struck deep into the northern shires of England. His own position having been weakened still further by his defeat at Bannockburn, Edward was unable to offer any support to the victims of this continuous aggression, and the Scots roamed at will, much as the Vikings had done centuries before, exacting tribute and laying waste tracts of Northumberland, County Durham and North Yorkshire.

In a sense, Robert's strategy could be interpreted as being essentially defensive in nature. While the plunder acquired in such raids was welcome, the English economy suffered only marginally as the main power base, in terms of trade, industry and agriculture, remained firmly rooted in the south. Scottish political and economic life, on the other hand, revolved around the lowlands, within striking distance of the border, thereby rendering Robert's dominance of the border country doubly important. Border raids, by both Scots and English, in what was to become known as 'reiver country', developed into a way of life, spanning 350 years.

Robert appreciated that border security depended very much on control of the great castles, such as Carlisle, Norham and Berwick. English occupation of the latter stronghold, the gateway to Scotland, was particularly irksome to Robert. Attempts to capture Carlisle in 1315 and Berwick in 1316 failed. Not until two years later, after an eleven-week siege, did Berwick finally capitulate – an act which finally persuaded Edward II to march north once more. In September 1319, even as he launched an assault on the walls of Berwick, the Scots were planning their most audacious raid to date, its objective the capture of Edward's queen, Isabella, who had been left at York. Learning of the plan, the Archbishop of York evacuated the royal retinue and, cobbling together a motley force, met the Scots under Sir James Douglas and the Earl of Moray a few miles from the city at Myton. The Archbishop's men were soundly thrashed and Edward was compelled to raise his siege of Berwick in order to prevent further depredations.

It was this latest fiasco which encouraged Edward to agree to a two-year truce. Although hostilities were, temporarily, at an end, Edward stubbornly refused to address Robert as King of Scotland, thereby leaving ajar the door to his claims on a land which he still viewed as a vassal state of his own kingdom.

The Walk

Distance: 7 miles (11.27 km)

One cannot rely on the Ordnance Survey Pathfinders in this instance, partly because the area of the battlefield and its approaches are covered by no less than three separate maps (Pathfinders 382, 383 and 393), making ready-reference rather difficult. In addition, on-going local enthusiasm for building new roads has rendered them sadly out of date. Hence, map references are limited. The recent (1995) issue of the Ordnance Survey atlas of West Central Scotland has rectified the situation to some extent, and the purchase of the pocket edition of this publication is recommended.

The starting point for the walk must be the National Trust for Scotland's Heritage Centre (Pathfinder 382–797906) (Point A), complete with a model of the battle and a fifteen-minute audio-visual presentation. The value of the 58 acre site owned by the Trust is largely symbolic, owing to the fact that the fighting occurred well to the north-east on land in the process of being engulfed by warehousing and distribution development. However, the landscaped grounds do include the Borestone (Pathfinder 382–795907) (literally, the 'bored stone' which held the Scottish standard) and Pilkington Jackson's famous bronze statue of the king, unveiled in 1964. Coxet Hill, to the rear of which the 'small folk' were hidden, is now covered with housing. The Bannock Burn runs to the south of the Heritage Centre. Between the river and the centre, in what is still open ground, was 'The Entry'. The Roman road by which the English vanguard approached New Park on 23 June stood to the west of the present-day Glasgow Road.

Leave the Heritage Centre, turning right into Glasgow Road. Continue down Glasgow Road, crossing the Bannock Burn and on to Pirnhall Road (Pathfinder 393–803892), following a zig-zag route to join the new ring road (the construction of which has left Bannockburn House marooned by

The Battle of Bannockburn, 1514

Monument to Robert the Bruce, King of Scotland, at the
National Trust for Scotland Heritage Centre.

the side of the M9 motorway). Follow the ring road up to the roundabout.
Crossing over, continue to follow the road (the A91) round as far as Station
Road (Point B). Turn into Station Road to follow the route taken by the
main English force to their camping ground. At some point, Clifford's
detachment swung westwards, along 'The Way' – a track running to the
west of the present-day railway line – to encounter the Earl of Moray's
infantry to the north-east of St Ninian's Church.

Follow Station Road to its junction with Stirling Road and turn left. At
the next roundabout (Point C), cross over (with care) to the A91
southbound carriageway and back-track a little way, using the right-hand
side grass verge. From the embankment, one has a remarkably good view of
the surrounding landscape. To the south-west, on a clear day, one can
discern the flagpole at the Heritage Centre, indicating the direction of the
Scots' advance on Edward II's army, deployed to north and south of the
present-day Stirling Road.

Return to the roundabout. To the north-east, between the Bannock Burn
and the River Forth, is the ground occupied by the English camp. The
English archers were deployed slightly to the north-west towards Loanhead,
by the Pelstream Burn. Turn to the left, to take the road – Kerse Road –
leading to the centre of Stirling. Turn left again, into Millhall Road

(Pathfinder 383–813924), following it through to Pike Road – and a new housing estate which forms the final link in a string of developments joining Bannockburn with Stirling. Cross the roundabout, a little way ahead and take Gillie's Drive into Shirra's Brae Road which leads onto Burghmuir Road (the A9) and St Ninian's (Pathfinder 382–796917), site of the preliminary action between Moray and Clifford. The parish church was rebuilt in 1751, the original structure having been accidentally blown apart while being used as an ammunition dump during the Jacobite rebellion of 1745–6 (see p. 128).

Finally, walk down Burghmuir Road, over the roundabout into Glasgow Road and so back to the starting point at the Heritage Centre.

Further Explorations

Stirling (Landranger 57–7993) holds much of interest for the military historian. In particular, one may take the opportunity to view the site of the Battle of Stirling Bridge at which, on 11 September 1297, William Wallace defeated the Earl of Surrey (see p. 2). Wallace and Sir Andrew de Moray deployed their force on the slopes of Abbey Craig (Pathfinder 383–810955). Surrey and Hugh de Cressingham, approaching from the west bank of the Forth, attempted to cross the river by the old bridge. This was not the surviving fifteenth-century stone foot-bridge ('Auld Brig') but a wooden structure located about half a mile further upstream (Pathfinder 382–785952) which could be used by just two horsemen at a time. Only half the English had crossed, when the Scots charged down from Abbey Craig. With those still on the west bank unable to reinforce them, the English on the east bank were cut to pieces. Only a few knights, among whom was Sir Marmaduke Tweng (see p. 9), were able to fight their way back to relative safety. Cressingham, leading the English vanguard, was killed, and his flayed skin used in the manufacture of a sword sheath for Wallace. Abbey Craig is identified by the Wallace Monument, a museum which includes Wallace's two-handed sword among its treasures.

Arguably, pride of place in any itinerary of Stirling must go to Stirling Castle (Pathfinder 382–790940). Situated on The Esplanade, leading up to the castle, is the Landmark Visitor Centre, with displays and audio-visual presentations describing Stirling's role in the development of the nation. Occupying a pivotal geographical position between north and south, Stirling Castle has been called 'the key to Scotland'. A fortress has occupied the site from the eleventh century but, in fulfilment of its role as a residence of the kings of Scotland, rebuilding has taken place over the centuries so that much of the surviving structure dates from the fifteenth and sixteenth centuries. During the Wars of Independence, it was reckoned to be the strongest castle in Scotland. The castle also had roles to play in the third and final act of the English Civil War, in 1651 and in the Jacobite Rebellion of 1745–6.

A third battle to take place in the locality was the Battle of Sauchieburn (Landranger 783868) fought in 1488 between James III and a strong confederation of rebels including the Home border clan, the 'Red' Douglases, the Earls of Angus and Argyll and the Bishop of Glasgow – against which the royal army proved to be no match. While making his escape from the field, James (who had armed himself with the sword of Robert I) was thrown from his horse. Carried to a nearby mill, he was stabbed to death by one of his enemies, posing as a priest. James was buried at Cambuskenneth Abbey (Pathfinder 383–807939). Founded in 1140 by King David I for the Augustinian order, Cambuskenneth occupies the possible site of yet another battle, between the first King of Scots, Kenneth MacAlpin (Kenneth I) and the Picts during the ninth century. The abbey was reduced to ruins in 1570 when the Earl of Mar (regent during the minority of James VI) decided to utilize the stone in the construction of a projected palace in Stirling, ruins of which, 'Mar's Wark', may be viewed in Castle Wynd.

Bannockburn House (Pathfinder 393–809889) was visited by Prince Charles Edward Stuart in January 1746. Staying there at the time was Clementina Walkinshaw, the niece of the owner, Sir Hugh Paterson. Clementina later became the prince's mistress, following him to France and bearing his daughter.

Menstrie Castle (Pathfinder 383–849968), built in the sixteenth century, was the home of the chiefs of the MacAlister clan, who changed their name to Alexander. Menstrie was the birthplace of Sir William Alexander, 1st Earl of Stirling and founder of Nova Scotia.

Further Information

Despite the proliferation of new roads to the south of Stirling, the Heritage Centre at Bannockburn, providing free car parking throughout the year, is well marked and easy to locate, lying on the A872 (Glasgow Road) just to the north of Junction 9 of the M9.

Travellers by rail should make for the mainline station of Stirling, which is well served by trains within Scotland and from south of the border, via both Midland and East Coast lines. For details of half-hourly Midland Bluebird bus services between Stirling railway station and Bannockburn, telephone 01324–613777. National Express (telephone 0990–808080) and Scottish Citylink (telephone 0990–505050) also operate coach services to Stirling.

Summer season opening times of the Vistior Centre are 10.00 a.m.–5.30 p.m. The centre can be very busy, and an early start is recommended. For up-to-date details of admission fees (£2.00 per adult in 1996), telephone the Resident Property Manager on 01786–812664.

In this most popular of tourist areas, tourist information offices abound. A visit to either the Tourist Information Centre situated at Junction 9 of the M9 Motorway Service Area (limited opening hours) or the Tourist Information Centre in Dumbarton Road, Stirling, is recommended. In order to make the most of a visit to any area, it is important to gather as much information as possible beforehand. In this respect, a very useful free *Visitor's Guide* – giving information on access to sites mentioned in the Further Explorations section, such as the Wallace Monument and Stirling Castle – is available. Write to the TIC, Dumbarton Road, Stirling or telephone 01786–475019.

As already indicated, accurate maps covering the area of the suggested walk are not easy to find. To begin with, the Heritage Centre occupies the extreme south-east corner of Pathfinder 382, and three Ordnance Survey Pathfinder maps: Pathfinder 383, 393 and 383 are required for the whole area. Ordnance Survey Landranger 57, while covering the area of the walk, is well out-of-date – so extensive has been redevelopment of the area over recent years. The best companion for the walk is the *Ordnance Survey Street Atlas of Glasgow & West Central Scotland* (pocket edition at £4.99) which also covers Kilsyth and Falkirk.

Much has been made of new roads encroaching upon English battlefields, such as Naseby and, currently (1996), Newbury, but the concrete jungle seems to be enveloping Bannockburn, unchallenged.

William Seymour's *Battles in Britain, Volume 1*, contains an account of the battle, illustrated with a useful aerial photograph. A 'must' for the serious student is W.M. Mackenzie's *The Battle of Bannockburn: A Study in Medieval Warfare*, first published in 1913, and re-issued by The Strong Oak Press Ltd in 1989. The National Trust for Scotland's own handbook: *Bannockburn* by Colonel Cameron Taylor, is available from the Heritage Centre.

2
THE BATTLE OF PINKIE
10 September 1547

Introduction

In the two centuries which had elapsed since Bannockburn, the relationship between Scotland and England in the mid-fourteenth century had not mellowed with the passage of time. The fighting which took place in the intervening years may be categorized as border warfare with an occasional hint of national rivalry. On 19 August 1388, for example, the great rival families of Douglas and Percy clashed at Otterburn in a battle which, although celebrated by contemporary balladeers, was essentially a parochial affair, with repercussions limited to the north of England. For an Anglo-Scottish battle on the scale of Bannockburn in terms of national and international significance, one has to move on to the Tudor age – to 9 September 1513 and the Battle of Flodden.

The Scots were never to recover from their devastating defeat on Flodden Field. Among the dead was their king, James IV, whose mutilated remains were discovered the day after the battle. His demise ushered in a prolonged period of instability, for his son and heir, also called James, was but a seventeen-month-old baby. Chief among those who struggled for power during the future James V's minority were his mother, the Queen Margaret (sister of Henry VIII of England), the pro-French Duke of Albany and the Douglas family.

The French influence was of some concern to Henry, and would remain so for the rest of his life. For his part, James – enthroned in 1528 at the age of sixteen – seemed quite happy to live with the 'Auld Alliance'. He enjoyed being cultivated by Francis I and his two French wives, Madeleine (who died shortly after her arrival in Scotland) and Mary each brought enormous dowries. Despite Henry's continuous efforts to improve relations with Scotland, James remained aloof. A meeting between the two monarchs, convened for 20 September 1541, failed to materialize, although Henry spent a week at York waiting for his nephew to appear.

The border fighting now began to gather momentum and, in August 1542, the Warden of the Middle Marches, Sir Robert Bowes, was captured in a skirmish at Hadden Ridge, between Kelso and Coldstream. In October of the same year, the Duke of Norfolk mounted a more successful raid, which led James to solicit the aid of his nobles for a major punitive expedition. With the disaster of Flodden still in living memory, support for the project was lukewarm, but with the help of Cardinal Beaton, arch-enemy of the English, James contrived to muster an army of 10,000 men. His favourite, Oliver Sinclair, a ne'er-do-well who had won the king's confidence, was placed in command. As soon as Sinclair crossed the border several bands, more interested in plunder than in death or glory, broke away from the main body – fortunate indeed for the Deputy Warden of the West Marches, Sir Thomas Wharton, who was unable to raise more than 3,000 men in the name of King Henry VIII.

On 24 November 1542, Wharton met up with the reduced expeditionary force at Solway Moss, an area of marshland near Gretna. Lacking firm leadership, the Scots were overwhelmed by Wharton's cavalry and driven into the marsh. Hundreds were slain and over 1,000 (including Sinclair) taken prisoner. It is said that the disappointment of this resounding defeat led to James's early death soon afterwards, at the age of thirty-one.

A further disappointment to the dying king had been the birth of a daughter, the future Mary Queen of Scots, instead of a much-needed son. However, this event did encourage the English to cease hostilities. The prisoners of Solway Moss, released from the Tower of London, were paid damages – the leading nobles receiving £200 each[1] – for Henry had now decided on a more diplomatic method of exerting his authority, with plans for a marriage between Mary and his own son, Prince Edward.

The Road to Pinkie

With the death of James V, Scotland was again reduced to turmoil. As with the period of her father's minority, so the years of Mary's minority were beset by courtly intrigue. James Hamilton, the Earl of Arran, was appointed regent, with Cardinal Beaton and James's widow, Queen Mary, heading a rival faction. As his first, unenviable, task, Arran had to respond to Henry VIII's peace proposals. Foremost among Henry's demands were requests

---

[1] Sinclair, by virtue of his lowly birth, received only £66 13s 4d.

that Mary should be sent to England to be raised as Prince Edward's future wife; that the castles of Edinburgh, Stirling and Dumbarton should be garrisoned by English troops, and that the pro-French Cardinal Beaton should be arrested and sent to England as a prisoner.

The Scottish response being somewhat slow in coming, Henry sent his envoy, Sir Ralph Sadleir, to assess the situation. Although Arran had been pleased to arrest Beaton, there was no suggestion that he be delivered into English hands. Indeed, he subsequently regained his liberty. Again, there was talk of the possibility of some English men and women residing with the infant Mary, but no agreement that she should leave Scotland. At length, the Scots were induced to meet Henry's terms by signing the Treaties of Greenwich, but the ink on the parchment had barely dried when Arran repudiated the agreement and restored the Auld Alliance.

Unable to check his fury at these developments, Henry despatched the Earl of Hertford to wage a campaign of terror, referred to as the 'Rough Wooing'. On 4 May 1544, Hertford landed at Leith, his army overcoming a force of 6,000 Scots led by Arran and Beaton. Both Leith and Edinburgh were laid waste, as were Dunbar and Jedburgh.

Border raids continued throughout the winter of 1544–5. Prominent among the English raiders, and acting largely upon his own initiative, was

The battlefield of Pinkie.

Sir Ralph Evers. In February 1545, Evers, at the head of 6,000 men – many of whom were European mercenaries – sacked Melrose and was about to move against Jedburgh when he was challenged by an inferior force of Scots commanded by the Earl of Angus. The problem created by men such as Evers was that they made no distinction between the Scottish nationalists and those Scots, such as Angus, who had been reasonably well-disposed towards the English. To Evers, all Scots, regardless of loyalties, were considered fair game, and the estates of Angus fared especially badly.

Evers, camped on Ancrum Moor, to the north of Jedburgh, was tempted into attacking Angus and Arran (shamed into joining his fellow countryman) who feigned a retreat. Having drawn the English on, the Scottish infantry turned to present an impenetrable wall of pikes on which Evers's horsemen were impaled. Quickly moving on to the offensive, the Scots scattered the mercenaries and put the entire army to flight. Evers himself was killed along with 800 of his followers. Flushed with their success, many of the less prudent victors of Ancrum Moor wanted to sweep into England, but were restrained by those who appreciated that a well-led, disciplined force might prove more difficult to overcome than Evers's raiders.

Nevertheless, with the French hatching a plot for an invasion of England, the Scots should have drawn up plans for, at the very least, a diversionary attack across the border at the appropriate time. The arrival in Scotland of some 5,000 French troops encouraged them to embark on what amounted to a series of very minor raids. The French invasion fleet having been repulsed at sea on 18 July 1545, Hertford was free to mount a devastating raid of his own. Over a dozen towns, including Melrose, were sacked and that year's harvest destroyed.

In the year 1546, both Scotland and England were beset by internal power struggles, leading, in Scotland, to the murder of Cardinal Beaton and, in England, to the indictment for high treason of the Earls of Norfolk and Surrey. When the failing Henry VIII died on 27 January 1547, the Earl of Hertford – as the Duke of Somerset – stepped in to claim the title of Protector of the Realm, during the minority of the ten-year-old Edward VI. One of Somerset's priorities was the enforcement of the provisions of the Treaties of Greenwich and, in particular, the marriage of Edward VI and Mary Queen of Scots, now five years of age. And so it came about that on 4 September 1547, Somerset, having raised an army of 16,000 men, prepared to leave Berwick to continue the 'rough wooing' policy of his late master.

On 6 September, having avoided Dunbar which he found to be strongly defended, Somerset reached Tantallon Castle, near North Berwick, and then moved on along the coastline via Longniddry to Prestonpans, from where he instructed the English fleet, sailing up the Firth of Forth in support of the invading army, to drop anchor at the mouth of the River Esk, at Musselburgh.

The Battle of Pinkie

On the west bank of the River Esk, about three miles from the English camp, was a Scottish army which Arran had amassed to protect the homeland, all internal bickering having been temporarily set aside in a display of unity against the common enemy. The wildest estimates put the strength of the Scots at 36,000 men, but 25,000 would be nearer the mark. Although they still vastly outnumbered the English, they were deficient in cavalry – totalling about 1,500 – and artillery. Somerset's force, on the other hand, included 4,000 cavalry and 80 cannon. In addition, the English commander could count on the support of his fleet, both in terms of firepower and as a means of evacuation, if necessary.

About a mile inland from Somerset's campsite, the ground rises sharply to Falside Hill and Carberry Hill, and it was along the lower slopes of the ridge that Somerset deployed his men. On the morning of 9 September, the Scottish cavalry of Lord Home crossed the Esk and cantered to and fro in a show of defiance before the English lines, daring the invaders to descend from their vantage point. Lord Grey's heavy cavalry obliged by charging into their midst and cutting them to pieces, thereby seriously compromising Arran's mobility in the field. It may well have been after this engagement that one side or the other proposed terms for a peaceful settlement. Accounts vary from the claim that Somerset offered to withdraw if the Scots would guarantee not to arrange an overseas marriage for Mary, to the suggestion that Arran proposed settling the dispute by combat between a select group of knights.

Neither option would have been acceptable and so – appreciative of the fact that the onus to attack lay with the English – on the morning of 10 September 1547, Somerset relinquished his vantage point to advance on the Scottish positions. Somerset with his second-in-command, the Earl of Warwick, took centre stage with the infantry, while the cavalry of Lord Grey and Sir Francis Brian occupied the right and left wings respectively. With the numerically superior Scots safely entrenched behind the Esk, it was a bold move. Had Arran remained in position, it could have proved disastrous for the English, whose surprise must have been great when they perceived the Earl of Argyll's Highlanders crossing the Esk to meet them.

Why the Scots acted as they did on what was to become known as 'Black Saturday', is a mystery. They may have been concerned that the English could take the high ground occupied by Inveresk Church, overlooking their lines, or they may have thought that Somerset had ordered a retreat to the transport ships. It is also possible that Arran was able to exert little authority over his allies and that the Highlanders, who may well have been taking a

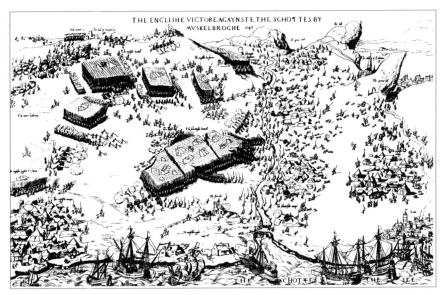

A contemporary engraving of the Battle of Pinkie. (Constance & Brian Dear)

heavy pounding from the English guns, surged forward on their own account.

Almost as big as mystery surrounds the inactivity of the English while Arran's substantial army, now committed to moving onto the offensive, crossed the Esk via a single, narrow bridge. Once on the west bank, they were able to form up in three battles, each comprising tightly packed ranks of pikemen. Although the final deployment is uncertain, Arran and Argyll would have occupied the centre ground, with (probably) the Earl of Angus on the right and the Earl of Huntley to the left. Somerset ordered Lord Grey's cavalry forward, but the impetus of the resulting charge was lost in the boggy ground surrounding a brook which lay between the English and Scottish lines – the Pinkie Cleugh from which the battle took its name. The pikes held firm and Grey, having suffered heavy losses, was compelled to retreat.

The Scottish rear ranks were being pummelled with cannon fire from the English fleet and now, with his heavy artillery in addition to his archers and arquebusiers in position, Somerset was able to wear down resistance. The cavalry having regrouped, another charge was launched at the noticeably thinning Scottish ranks, and this time they gave way. Taking flight, many were caught crowding onto the bridge while others, dispensing with their armour, flung themselves into the Esk. It is said that Arran was among the first to quit the field. In the heat of victory, it was now Somerset who was unable to control his men as they slaughtered the panic-stricken foe. The standard preferred practice of taking prisoners for ransom was abandoned in a demonstration of blood-lust which claimed 10,000 Scottish lives.

The Aftermath

At their own estimate, the English lost barely sixty dead. A more realistic estimate at anywhere between 200 and 500 dead would still mean that English casualties were light, having been sustained mainly during the heavy cavalry charges. Many on both sides were wounded, including Lord Grey. Had Somerset not put a 5 mile limit on the pursuit and a 6.00 p.m. time limit on looting, the carnage among the Scots would doubtless have been much greater.

The following day, Somerset marched to Leith and on to Holyrood which was ravaged once more. The English fleet, sailing on to Dundee, took Broughty Castle and established a valuable outpost on the island of Inchkeith, commanding the entrance to the Firth of Forth. Although the Scottish Council, safely ensconced at Stirling, agreed to send representatives to peace negotiations at Berwick within two weeks, they knew that Somerset would soon have to disband his army, which he did on 29 September. The Earl of Warwick and Lord Grey, deputed to enter into negotiations with the Scots, must have suspected that their wait at Berwick would be futile – as, indeed, it was.

In the long term, the English victory achieved very little and in some respects was counter-productive. Far from securing the union of Mary and Edward, it had served only to strengthen Franco-Scottish ties. After Pinkie, the young queen had been taken for safety from Stirling to Inchmahome Priory on an island in the Lake of Menteith. The following year, she was moved to Dumbarton from which port she sailed for France, where she spent the next thirteen years, marrying the Dauphin – the future Francis II – in April 1558.

The Battle of Pinkie also confirmed that the Scots were no longer any match for the up-do-date English army, and they were happy to reinforce their own depleted ranks by accommodating 7,000 French troops. As it turned out, the latter outstayed their welcome, remaining in Scotland for eight years and leading many Scots to wonder whether, in terms of maintaining their independence, they were much better off.

Upon his return to London, Somerset had received a hero's welcome but, like many a successful general before and since, his undoubted military talents failed to match his ability to cope with the politics of peacetime. His enthusiasm for the Reformation alienated traditionalists, and in the year 1549, armed insurrections sprang up in many parts of the kingdom. In the west country, a peasant army hovered menacingly before the gates of Exeter, while in the east, largely as a response to the land enclosure programme, a substantial force under the leadership of Robert Kett, gathered on Mousehold Heath, near Norwich.

In the face of these problems, and turning to the scene of earlier successes, Somerset began to think about another invasion of Scotland. He had got so far as to despatch in the direction of the border, an army composed mainly of German and Italian mercenaries under the command of the Earl of Warwick. However, the situation in Norwich had deteriorated to such an extent that Warwick's attention was diverted there. The rebellion was quelled and Kett hanged.

Such disorders were not lost on the French, who exploited them by marching on – and taking – Boulogne, which Henry VIII had captured in 1544. The subsequent Treaty of Bologne led to England's surrender both of her remaining French possessions and the loss of her foothold in eastern Scotland. All within the space of two years, such benefits as Somerset had gained for England on the battlefield of Pinkie had disappeared.

The Walk

Distance: 6½ miles (10.47 km)

Begin in Inveresk, near the National Trust for Scotland's Inveresk Lodge Garden (Pathfinder 407–348718) (Point A). There is ample car parking space along Inveresk Village Road – the A6124. Walk in a south-easterly direction, taking Crookston Road, which branches off Inveresk Village Road to the left. As one approaches the railway bridge, the landscape opens up, to reveal an expanse of level ground to the left and, in front, 2 miles away, the eminence of Falside Hill, capped by Falside Castle. The Scots would have swarmed across the area to the left and right of the small hump-backed bridge, hurrying to their doom at Barbachlaw.

Continue walking up the road which once led directly to the hamlet of Crookston, but which, like many another minor road, has been severed by the development of the A1. Walk up the cycle track below the slip road, to join the footpath on Salter's Road (Pathfinder 407–363713) and turn to the right so as to cross the A1 dual carriageway running beneath.

Once across, take the minor road on the left for Crookston to begin what develops into a steep ascent of Falside Hill. Falside Castle (Pathfinder 407–378710) (Point B) actually occupies an eminence slightly to the south-west of the hill itself, but the site nevertheless affords splendid views over Musselburgh and the battlefield. For 500 years, the 'castle' was home to the Fawsyde family who annoyed Somerset's men with arquebus fire. After the battle, the structure was put to the torch, the incumbents being 'brent and smoothered within'. In fact, Falside is a tower house – the poor man's castle – of which East Lothian has many interesting examples.

A mile away to the south of Falside is Carberry Hill (Landranger 66 36 69), scene of a confrontation between forces led by the Earl of Bothwell and Mary, Queen of Scots, and rebel nobles who opposed their marriage. In the event, at the first threat of attack, the royal army abandoned its hilltop position – within earthworks hastily thrown up by Somerset on the eve of the Battle of Pinkie twenty years earlier – and took to its heels.

After resting, return to Crookston, noting that the lower slopes of Falside Hill, to left and right of one's route, were occupied by the English army. At the junction, turn right to follow Salter's Road. Continue to the track to the left (Pathfinder 407–365716) leading to the sewage works and signposted by the Scottish Rights of Way Society. Skirting the building which seems to block one's path approaching the works site, negotiate the railway line by means of the underpass and continue on to the built-up area – probably the scene of some of the heaviest fighting of the battle. Turn into Pinkie Terrace and at the top, bear left into Pinkie Road. Continue walking and Pinkie House soon becomes visible in the school grounds on the opposite side of the road (Pathfinder 407–349727), a marker for the probable site of the Scottish left wing.

Continue along Pinkie Road and on into Inveresk Road, turning left to proceed up Church Lane, just beyond St Michael's Avenue. The church, somewhat obscured from the front, does not appear to occupy a very prominent position. However, when one climbs the steps at the end of Church Lane, its height becomes only too apparent. The present-day Church of St Michael itself (Pathfinder 407–345721) (Point C) dates from 1803, although there is evidence of the site having being a place of worship since around AD 500.

One of the benefits of rambling for the individual is a broadening of interests – in houses and gardens, for example. And, as one proceeds from St Michael's Church back to the starting point, one cannot fail to be struck by the awesome parade of fine seventeenth and eighteenth-century mansions comprising Inveresk village. Set back from the road and sheltered by high stone walls, each is sufficient to engender admiration its own right. The oldest is Inveresk Lodge and a tour of the terraced gardens, open to the public, constitutes a fine conclusion to the walk.

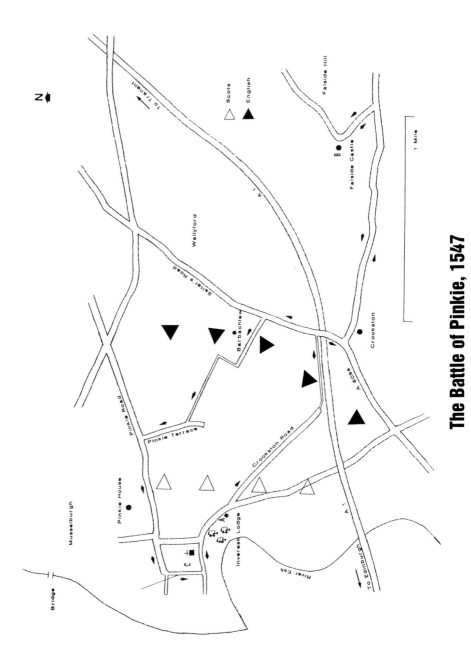

The Battle of Pinkie, 1547

Further Explorations

The cover of Ordnance Survey Pathfinder 407 depicts Musselburgh, Leith and Edinburgh as separate entities, but on the ground the three are indivisible. Leith was devoured by Edinburgh in 1920, and only the burgh signs enable one to distinguish where Edinburgh ends and Musselburgh begins. With the centres of Edinburgh and Musselburgh only 5 miles apart, a visit to the site of the Battle of Pinkie may be supported by visits to selected places of interest in the nation's capital.

There are two sites of particular interest to the battlefield historian. One of these is Holyrood (Pathfinder 407–275735), site of Holyrood Abbey and Holyrood Palace. Founded in 1128 by King David I, the Augustinian Abbey became a court residence. James II was crowned here and although, as noted earlier, the English wrought much damage in the mid-1540s, the abbey church was able to stage the coronation of Charles I in 1633. Holyrood Palace, building of which was begun in 1500 around the abbey guest house, eventually replaced the abbey as a royal residence. Queen Mary lived here for six years, and visitors may view the apartments occupied by herself and her second husband, Lord Darnley. A plaque marks the spot where the jealous Darnley murdered Mary's secretary, David Rizzio. In 1650, during the latter days of the English Civil War, Cromwell's army used the palace as winter quarters and in 1745, the 'Young Pretender' ('Bonnie Prince Charlie' or 'Charles III' depending upon one's point of view) held court here. The strategic importance of Holyrood goes back, in fact, much further in time with identifiable earthworks and Iron Age hillforts, notably Arthur's Seat (Pathfinder 407–275727) and Dunsapie (Pathfinder 407–282732).

The second essential place of pilgrimage is Edinburgh Castle (Pathfinder 407–252735). As with Holyrood, this splendid vantage point must once have appealed to Iron Age settlers, and although fortifications have adorned the site ever since, the castle does not enter fully into recorded history until the eleventh century, when it was considered suitable as a residence for King Malcolm III. The chapel built by Malcolm's English queen, Margaret, survives as a reminder of this period. During the Wars of Independence, much of the castle as it then stood was slighted by Robert the Bruce and rebuilt in the fourteenth century by David II.

Over the centuries, Edinburgh Castle has withstood many sieges. During the English Civil Wars, it changed hands on several occasions and after falling to Cromwell in 1650, housed an English garrison until the Restoration. Cromwell had tried to undermine the defences by tunnelling into the crag on the south side, but as the volcanic rock proved impervious to his attempts, the project was abandoned. Indentations resulting from this activity can still be discerned. When Cromwell took the castle, he discovered, amongst the artillery, 'Mons Meg', a cannon made in Belgium in 1449 and presented to James II by the Duke of Burgundy. Weighing nearly 4 tons and with a calibre of 20 in, she was capable of firing stone cannonballs of 300 lb in weight. James used the cannon in his struggle against the Douglases in 1455, when it was certainly used in the siege of the Douglas stronghold of Threave Castle. It may be viewed today in Edinburgh Castle's vaults.

Outside the castle, on Castlehill, is Cannonball House, so named because a cannonball is embedded in the west gable. It was fired during the '45 Rebellion, the last occasion on which the castle was attacked.

Further Information

By road, Musselburgh is best approached from the south, via the A6124. The best day for the motorist to visit is Sunday. Any attempts to negotiate the north side of the town on a weekday is likely to end in failure. Anyone who goes astray should look out for National Trust for Scotland signs to Inveresk Lodge Gardens – the starting point for the suggested walk.

The initial objective for rail travellers is Edinburgh. A local service, operating between Edinburgh and North Berwick, will take one on to Musselburgh (telephone 0131–556–2451). It should be noted that the railway station is inconveniently situated well to the south-west of the town. For details of bus services linking Edinburgh and Musselburgh, telephone 0131–225–3858.

The battlefield has no monument and no information for visitors is available – an omission which the excellent East Lothian Tourist Board will no doubt rectify in due course. A Tourist Information Centre is situated at the Old Craighhall Service Area on the A1 (telephone 0131–653–6172).

An additional day is required for optional visits to Holyrood and Edinburgh Castle. For up-to-date information on opening times and entry fees in respect of Edinburgh Castle, call Historic Scotland's enquiry line on 0131–668–8800. For visitor information concerning Holyrood, call 0131–556–1096.

Ordnance Survey Pathfinder 407 and Landranger 66 are the relevant maps. Further reading is limited, but William Seymour's *Battles in Britain 1066–1547* includes an account, illustrated with aerial photographs. Howard Green's *Guide to the Battlefields of Britain and Ireland* also has a useful chapter on the battle. Green's book, out of print for many years, can still be obtained through libraries and/or via the inter-library loan system. Green took the trouble to make a detailed exploration of every battlefield about which he wrote, and it is interesting to note that the field of Pinkie Heugh, unlike most, has changed very little in the twenty-five years which have passed since his visit.

3
THE BATTLE OF AULDEARN
9 May 1645

Introduction

By the late summer of 1643, the English Civil War had been raging for almost one year, with neither side – Royalists nor Roundheads – making much progress at the expense of the other. The Royalists, it may be argued, were ahead on points, with victories that summer in the south (Roundway Down), the south-west (Stratton), the midlands (Chalgrove Field) and the north (Adwalton Moor). In addition, after a siege of only three days, Bristol had surrendered to Prince Rupert on 26 July. Following these reversals, leading Parliamentarian, John Pym, grew particularly anxious to win the support of the Scots for the Parliamentary cause.

As one might imagine, opinion in Scotland was divided but, recognizing that they were in a position to drive a hard bargain, the Scottish Parliament's Committee of the Three Estates set a heavy price on the sale of their loyalty. The English Parliament had hoped for a straight-forward military alliance, but the Scots imposed conditions for religious reforms which, although acceptable to the essentially Presbyterian Roundheads, would not be sympathetically viewed by the rest of the country. 'The Solemn League and Covenant' (as it was known) between Scotland and England provided for the extirpation of Roman Catholicism and the preservation of the reformed religion (i.e. the Presbyterian Church) in England and Ireland. The rights of Parliament were to be upheld and all opponents of the League to be suppressed. As far as the English Parliament was concerned, the problem of imposing Presbyterianism throughout England and Ireland could be addressed later. For now, the agreement had the desired effect leading, in mid-January 1644, to a Scottish army of over 20,000 men commanded by the Earl of Leven, crossing the border into England.

Among the Scots who refused to support the Solemn League and Covenant was James Graham, Marquis of Montrose. Originally a leader of the Scottish nationalist movement, Montrose felt that the provisions of the

Solemn League went too far. With some justification, Montrose argued that the League compromised freedom of choice and claimed that in taking up arms against their king, the Scots – like the English – would be guilty of high treason. Perhaps in view of his earlier nationalistic sentiments, Charles I reacted with some reserve towards his offer of support. However, when the impotence of the leader of the royalist faction in Scotland, the King's commissioner, the Marquis of Hamilton, became apparent, Charles had little choice but to turn to his new ally. Unlike most of the English landed gentry who fought on the Royalist side, Montrose possessed no great personal wealth on which he could draw in order to equip and field a body of troops, but he was ultimately given the title of Lieutenant-Governor and Captain-General over all the king's forces in Scotland.

In conference with Charles at Oxford, Montrose suggested that he should concentrate on raising forces in border country while the Earl of Antrim recruited an Irish army to invade Scotland from the west. Montrose hoped that the Marquis of Newcastle would be able to furnish him with sufficient troops to form the nucleus of an army but Newcastle, himself hard pressed by Leven, was able to let him have only 100 regular troops, and at the head of these, the captain-general set off to Carlisle. On the way, he was able to pick up some 800 men of the Cumberland and Westmoreland militias, but as soon as he crossed the border on 13 April 1644, many of them deserted, so that by the time he reached Dumfries to await news of Antrim's Irish army, his numbers had dwindled to a few hundred. Rapidly approaching Covenant troops forced him to retreat into England and to Newcastle's current base at Durham.

At last seeing the value of encouraging Montrose's ambitions, Newcastle lent him 2,000 infantry and 500 cavalry hoping, in so doing, that he would at least succeed in creating a diversion. Unfortunately, Leven had captured and garrisoned Morpeth Castle, which had to be taken en route. Montrose stormed the town on 29 May after a siege lasting twenty days, but his biographers, while listing this action among his successes, do tend to ignore the negative aspects of the campaign, for although he went on to take South Shields, he was repulsed at Sunderland, and one is tempted to argue that the troops thus tied down in the north-east might have been better employed in contributing to the Royalist effort at the forthcoming Battle of Marston Moor.

The Road to Auldearn

On 2 July 1644, the combined armies of Sir Thomas Fairfax, the Earl of Manchester and the Earl of Leven overwhelmed the Royalists at Marston Moor, near York. After the battle, Prince Rupert made his way northward,

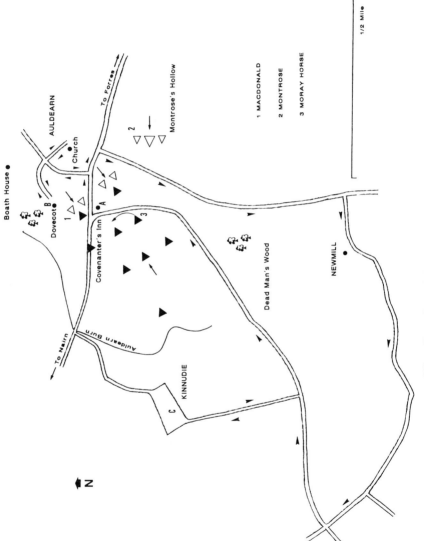

The Battle of Auldearn, 1645

to Thirsk, and thence to Richmond where, on 4 July, he met Montrose who, somewhat tardily, was on his way south. Instead of reinforcing Montrose, as the Marquis had hoped, Rupert relieved him of his own regulars, leaving him to make his way back home as best he could.

At first, Montrose's efforts to gather an army to further the Royalist cause were unsuccessful. However, the Earl of Antrim, who initially had experienced similar difficulties in Ireland, had managed to persuade the fearless warrier, Alasdair MacDonald, to lead a motley force of 1,000 men across the Irish Sea. MacDonald's family having been ousted from their homeland by the Campbells, Alasdair viewed the adventure largely as an opportunity to gain revenge. On 27 June 1644, this Catholic army, ostensibly raised to bolster the Protestant cause, set sail, finally joining up with Montrose in late August at Truidh Hill.

The first trial of strength took place at Tibbermore, to the west of Perth. Here, on 1 September 1644, an army of between 6,000 and 7,000 Covenanters, led by David Wemyss, Lord Elcho, opposed the Royalist advance on the town. Elcho's force was divided into three: the Earl of Tullibardine in the centre, with Sir James Scott on the left and Elcho himself on the right. Both flanks enjoyed the protection of cavalry. Montrose, for whom recruitment was still slow, was unable to field more than 3,000 men, yet he matched Elcho's deployment by placing MacDonald in the centre, John Graham, Lord Kilpont, on the left and himself on the right. Elcho expected a cavalry charge to disperse Kilpont's divisions, but they held firm and although fierce fighting occurred on the Royalist right between Montrose and Scott, MacDonald led a charge which broke the Covenanters' centre ranks leading to a wholesale retreat. Over 1,000 were slaughtered in the pursuit, while precious supplies, including much-needed arms and ammunition, fell into Royalist hands.

With the Earl of Argyll hurrying eastward, Montrose abandoned Perth almost immediately and, unable to cower Dundee into submission, he made for Aberdeen, gathering more adherents on the way, in particular, eighty or so invaluable cavalrymen. Defending Aberdeen was a numerically strong – about 6,000 men – though poorly led army of regulars, militia and levies. The resulting clash at Justice Mills unfolded in much the same way as the fight at Tibbermore, with desperate encounters taking place on both wings as MacDonald pressed inexorably forward in the centre. Although accounts of the battle vary, it is agreed that MacDonald was responsible for the most impressive manoeuvre of the battle when his Irishmen seemingly gave way before a Covenanter cavalry charge led by Sir William Forbes of Craigievar, only to close ranks behind the hapless troopers once they were in their midst.

The fighting raged for at least two hours, until the Covenanters, lacking firm leadership, gave way. On this occasion, the pursuit developed into a monstrous four-day rape of the city, an act which sullied Montrose's reputation for ever. Afterwards, in extenuation, it was claimed that the Irish had been unleashed on the citizens as a punishment for the shooting of a Royalist drummer accompanying a peace envoy into Aberdeen prior to the commencement of the battle. The probability is that he was unable to control the excesses of the Irish, whose future mobility was seriously hampered, weighed down as they were with the fruits of looting.

With Argyll constantly threatening his position, Montrose was kept on the move, but with the approach of the harsh Scottish winter, the prospect of a third major confrontation rescinded. While Montrose wanted to retreat to the lowlands, however, MacDonald was keen to move west to attack the hated Campbells. He argued that in doing so, Montrose would be striking a blow in the very heart of Argyll country. In any event, he threatened to go home if he did not get his own way. Thus, unwillingly, Montrose embarked on a winter campaign of guerilla warfare in which many Campbells were slaughtered, and which culminated in the Battle of Inverlochy. There, on 2 February 1645, the Covenanters under Argyll, yet again outnumbering the Royalists by two to one, were routed. As at Justice Mills, Montrose could not prevent a vigorous pursuit resulting in the slaughter of 1,500 of the enemy.

From Inverlochy, the Royalists proceeded by way of the south side of Loch Ness, by-passing Inverness to descend on Elgin which, despite buying protection for the sum of £1,300, was torched. Now plundering at will and thereby depriving itself of prospective sympathy and support, the army continued along the coast to Banff, where it turned south to Turriff. The capture in Aberdeen of a careless troop of Royalist horse commanded by Nathaniel Gordon led to another reprisal raid on the city while Montrose, with the main body of the army, moved on via Stonehaven to Fettercairn, 10 miles to the north of Montrose. Having learned that Charles I planned to join him, he was hoping to continue southward, but found his path blocked at Dunkeld by General William Baillie who, following Argyll's failure, had been appointed supreme commander of Covenanter forces in Scotland.

Determined to turn the situation to advantage, Montrose made a forced march to Dundee, covering the 26 miles between Dundee and Dunkeld in fourteen hours. He launched his assault on 4 April 1645, and although everything went well at first, many of the Irish, failing to keep their minds on the task in hand, fell to looting thereby giving the garrison an opportunity to organize itself into holding out until relieved. Relief duly arrived in the person of Lieutenant-Colonel John Hurry, a notorious turncoat whose saving grace, as far as the Royalists were concerned, was that he did not get on well with his commander-in-chief, Baillie. Yet, despite Baillie's complaints that Hurry defied his orders, the latter did succeed in surprising and putting to flight the Royalist army, inflicting upon Monstrose his first defeat. A further forced march took the Royalists to temporary safety in Glen Esk, their numbers depleted by Hurry's relentless harassment.

Unabashed at this reversal, Montrose stepped up his on-going recruitment drive almost immediately. Stealing back to Dunkeld, he found that new adherents were, if anything, harder to attract than hitherto although he was cheered to some extent by the acquisition of James Gordon (Viscount Aboyne) and the young Lord Napier. Receiving intelligence that Hurry was active to the north, ravaging Gordon country, Montrose made another forced march aiming to reduce the pressure on his beleaguered allies. By 30 April, he had reached Skene, 7 miles to the west of Aberdeen, where he was joined by Alasdair MacDonald together with Lord Gordon and more reinforcements. As the Royalists advanced, so Hurry retreated before them, drawing them on into hostile territory until, on the evening of 8 May, Montrose made camp at the village of Auldearn, a little over 2 miles to the east of Nairn.

The Battle of Auldearn

Evidently, this was the moment for which Hurry, encamped at Inverness, was waiting. Having been reinforced to an extent which enabled him to field some 3,500 infantry and 400 horse, he felt confident of transforming his own position from the hunted into that of the hunter. A night march in heavy rain should have enabled him to surprise his prey, but as he approached, his musketeers tested their damp weapons by firing them, thus alerting Montrose to their approach.

Accustomed to reacting quickly, the Royalists were able to deploy before Hurry's arrival. Despite being able to muster only 2,000 infantry and 250 horse, Montrose made the astonishing decision to divide his command. MacDonald, with 500 men, took up a position to the north of the village along a front of about 400 yards in length and bounded on the right by the present-day Castle Hill, while Montrose, with the main body of his force – including the newly acquired cavalry of Gordon and Aboyne – assumed a concealed position to the east.

Advancing from the south-west, Hurry took up a strong position on Garlic Hill, where he remained with most of his cavalry. If anything, his force was too numerous for what he thought was the task in hand as, unaware of Montrose's position, he funnelled his men into a narrow front to face MacDonald's entrenched positions before the Royal Standard. In the van were the infantry regiments of the Earl of Loudon and Sir Mungo Campbell of Lawers; immediately to the rear were the regiments of the Earls

James Graham, Marquis of
Montrose. (Mary Evans Picture
Library)

of Lothian and Buchanan, supported by the Moray Horse. Between these divisions and Hurry's own reserve stood a contingent of northern levies, flanked by infantry regiments of the Earls of Sutherland and Seaforth.

As the infantry of Lawers and Loudon advanced, MacDonald rashly charged out to meet them but, notwithstanding their undoubted courage, his men were overwhelmed and driven back by sheer weight of numbers. To save them from extinction, Montrose was compelled to unleash Gordon's horse. The crucial manoeuvre of the battle now occurred as Moray's advancing cavalry wheeled-in to their left, to fall back on their own lines. It is said that the commander of Moray's horse, Captain Drummond, either misinterpreted an order from Hurry or himself gave the wrong order to his men, but the unexpected sight of Gordon's cavalry bearing down upon them may have been sufficient, in itself, to cause them to sheer away. Aboyne's horse followed up Gordon's charge against the Covenanters' right wing which, without the protection of Moray's horse, lay open to attack.

Had the Covenanters kept their heads, they could have retained the upper hand. MacDonald's charge – the centrepiece of all Montrose's victories – had been contained but Hurry still held 250 cavalry in reserve. In the end, it may well have been the northern levies who panicked as the Royalist horse and infantry burst into the arena. Certainly, heavy fighting continued for some time with Lawer's and Lothian's foot, Sir Mungo Campbell among them, dying where they stood after MacDonald rallied his men for a renewed assault.

On a field of battle as confined as that of Auldearn, it was natural that confusion should result when the Covenanters' right wing was turned in upon the centre. The degree of confusion would have been such as to preclude Hurry from effectively deploying his cavalry and, with the benefit of hindsight, he may have wished that more of them had been utilized in the support of his infantry at the outset. As it was, the commitment of the Royalist infantry eventually wore down the resolve of the Covenanters in the rear, many of whom on the left wing would not have been able to strike a blow while the fighting was at its height. In the end, they sought to save themselves, leaving Montrose in occupation of the field. Hurry, belying his name, was one of the last to flee, doubtless considering it his duty to preserve what he could of his cavalry.

The Aftermath

The fleeing Covenanters were pursued as far as Inverness, suffering heavy casualties along the way. Montrose put the final total of Covenanter dead at 3,000. Other more realistic estimates – horrendous enough in themselves – vary between 1,000 and 2,000. Again, sources sympathetic to Montrose put Royalist losses at a mere handful, although they must have been in the order of three figures, MacDonald's men alone having taken severe punishment in the opening round of the battle.

The battle itself is universally regarded as a 'classic', and Montrose's greatest victory. In his *Battles & Generals of the Civil Wars*, Colonel Rogers goes so far as to describe it as 'the most brilliant battle of the whole Civil War'. However, one might suggest that the outcome could have been very different, if only Moray's Horse had held firm. Certainly, their commander, Captain Drummond, was made the scapegoat for Hurry's defeat, being tried, condemned and shot in unseemly haste. The true culprit was Hurry himself for, in his anxiety to win glory, he failed to wait for his superior, Baillie, to join him before launching his attack. As time would show, the only sure way to beat the Royalists, would be to overwhelm them by sheer weight of numbers.

The Covenanters' loss in terms of available fighting men was not great, for Baillie still had at his disposal 2,000 infantry and several hundred horse, while recruitment would always be a far easier process for Baillie than it would be for Montrose. Although the Royalists were winning battles, they were fighting a very defensive war and, in their hand-to-mouth existence, the supplies they captured after a victory would prove invaluable. So, in the present instance, Hurry's baggage train was eagerly pillaged. The downside of the windfall was that many Royalist Highlanders tended to view the capture of enemy booty as the objective of the campaign and, once enriched, made their way home, thus exacerbating Montrose's manpower problem.

Montrose tarried at Auldearn for two precious days, thus relinquishing another opportunity to take the initiative with a rapid march on Inverness. Instead, he went east, to Elgin, where his wounded were cared for, while Baillie, suitably reinforced, marched to Huntley. Apparently, Hurry's defeat at Auldearn had cooled his ardour for, to Baillie's gratification, he sought temporary retirement on the grounds of ill-health.

There now followed an interlude in which both parties, like wary boxers assessing the strength of an opponent, stalked one another. Unlike earlier conflicts in which, generally speaking, priority was given to engaging one's enemy at the earliest opportunity, the Civil War, north and south of the border, committed the participants to thousands of miles of strategic (though often seemingly aimless) marches – and, consequently, in heavy expenditure in terms of time, effort and resources. Thus, with Montrose on the move again and approaching Huntley via Fochbars and Keith, the battle which, in the past, would have taken place on 22 May at Huntley, was avoided as Montrose swung westwards to Balvenie and then south to Corgarff Castle and Abernethy. While the Royalists were surviving by plundering provisions as they marched, the Covenanters were running desperately short of supplies and Baillie found it necessary to return to Inverness, leaving Montrose free to attempt to negotiate an exchange of prisoners with Argyll, at Blair Atholl.

By 3 June, Baillie was back in the field, to find that Montrose had made an abortive excursion to Inverquharty Castle, near Forfar, where the Earl of Lindsay was recruiting for the Covenanters. Wisely, Lindsay retreated and although the Royalists now had to live with the prospect of a Covenanter army to their rear, they had at least succeeded in driving Lindsay and Baillie further apart. Returning to Corgarff Castle, Montrose was met by Lord Gordon and MacDonald who had succeeded in encouraging some of the AWOL Highlanders to return to the fold, enabling the Royalists to march north to meet with Baillie and their next adventure.

The Walk

Distance: 4 miles (6.44 km)

Begin in the village of Auldearn, at the Covenanters' Inn (Pathfinder 161–917554) (Point A). Originally a mill existing at the time of the battle – and therefore a useful point of reference – the building was converted into an inn in 1973. Walk east along High Street and turn into Boath Road. At the top of Boath Road, turn left into Doocot Road, and on to the seventeenth-century dovecote (Pathfinder 161–917556) (Point B). On this high ground – known locally as Castle Hill – occupied by Alasdair Macdonald, Montrose raised his standard. It is still a splendid viewpoint from which, with the aid of the battle plan provided, one may easily visualize the action. To the north is Boath House (Pathfinder 161–919558), where Montrose allegedly spent the night after the battle.

Walk back down Doocot Road and into Boath Road. Opposite the police station, turn left to arrive at Auldearn parish church (Pathfinder 161–919556). The present building was erected in 1757 on the foundations of the original church which figured prominently in the trials of Scotland's most famous witch, Isobel Gowdie. It was here that Isobel claimed to have met the Devil. During her examination, which also took place in the church in March 1662, she claimed to have had 'carnal copulation and dealing with' Satan, and to have indulged in various nefarious practices and rituals aimed at the destruction of individuals and the blighting of crops. In July 1662, Isobel was committed for trial and although there is no record of the outcome, it is believed locally that the defendant was burned at the stake and her ashes buried nearby.

After this diversion, continue down Boath Road, turning left into High Street by The Lion, an inn since the early eighteenth century, before turning right into Lethen Road. The area to the left, where Montrose lay in wait for the impetuous Hurry, is still known locally as Montrose's Hollow. Further along Lethen Road, to the right, is Dead Man's Wood (Pathfinder 161–916548), burial place for most of the fallen. Continue to the single track road leading to Newmill. Take this road and follow it around as far as Grigorhill, at which point it crosses the B9101 (Pathfinder 161–905546). Turn right and proceed as far as the track leading to Kinnudie (Pathfinder 161–911547).

By walking up this track as far as the estate (Pathfinder 161–909551) (Point C), one may view the battleground from the Covenanters' position, for it was in the vicinity of Kinnudie that Hurry deployed his force, which advanced to take up its final position on Garlic Hill – Hurry himself remaining in the rear with his cavalry reserve, which was to flee without engaging the enemy. The land, it will be observed, is no longer marshy and, as with many battlefields, it is also undulating. Return to the road to continue walking towards Auldearn. The bend in the road (Pathfinder 161–917552), just to the south of the village, is identified by the battle plan on Castle Hill as the spot where Montrose's cavalry, having broken cover, forced Moray's Horse to turn in upon their own lines. Continue walking back to the Covenanters' Inn, which must mark the very centre of the battlefield.

It is sometimes claimed that the Battle of Auldearn is difficult to envisage owing to changes in the landscape. As already noted, the well-drained ground crossed by the Auldearn Burn (Pathfinder 161–913552) is no longer boggy. Similarly, as one might expect, the configuration of the local roads has changed. Most notably, the stretch of the A96 between The Lion and the spot to the south of Auchnacloich (Pathfinder 161–904562) did not exist at the time of the battle. Additionally, the village itself seems to have been limited to the immediate area of The Lion. However, the area in which the action took place is quite compact and, had all battlefields remained so comparatively undisturbed as that of Auldearn, one would have little cause for complaint.

Further Explorations

The town nearest to Auldearn, just 2 miles away, is Nairn (Landranger 27 8856). Once the seat of the Thane of Cawdor and the site of a castle which has long since disappeared, Nairn was a centre of commerce as early as the twelfth century. James VI once remarked that folk who lived at one end of the town were unable to understand the language spoken by the inhabitants of the other end – a veiled reference to the claim that the Highland Line intersects the High Street.

As a glance at the Ordnance Survey map will show, the area is rich in castles, both complete and ruined. Rait Castle (Pathfinder 161 894525), falling within the former category, dates from the fifteenth century. The Duke of Cumberland reputedly stayed here en route to Culloden. Rait Castle is sometimes identified as the scene of the legendary massacre of the Comyns by the Mackintoshes. In fact, the Mackintoshes, who had been invited to a feast at the Castle, were the intended victims but, having been forewarned, they turned the tables on their sly hosts. The Comyn chief, suspecting his daughter of betraying her kin, cut off her hands as she dangled from a window in an attempt to escape her father's wrath. Her ghost reputedly haunts the castle. The problem with this story is that it is also often told in connection with Cawdor Castle (see below) and the long-vanished Raits Castle near Kingussie – a cautionary tale for all who lack an uncritical eye.

Four miles to the east of Auldearn is Brodie Castle (Pathfinder 161 980578), also dating from the fifteenth century, on land owned by the Brodie family since the eleventh century. Much of the original building was destroyed by Lord Gordon during Montrose's campaigns, but sufficient survived to facilitate a restoration programme, with subsequent nineteenth-century additions.

From Brodie Castle, a journey of another 4 miles along the A96 brings one to Forres (Landranger 27 0358). There is some evidence to suggest that a settlement existed here in Roman times, and a medieval castle, though no longer in existence, is another signpost to the historical importance of the town. King Donald Bane was killed at Forres in the year 900, and Shakespeare identifies Forres as town to which Macbeth and Banquo are travelling when they meet with the three witches. The 'blasted heath' is traditionally identified with Macbeth's Hillock (Landranger 27–9656), to the west of Brodie Castle. In addition to a monument, erected in 1806, to Lord Nelson, Forres has a far more imposing monument, Sueno's Stone, which stands to the east of the town (Landranger 27–0459), erected in the ninth century in commemoration of a victory over Norse invaders.

For another site with a Macbeth connection, one has to turn 6 miles to the west of Auldearn, to Cawdor Castle (Landranger 27–8449), seat of the Thanes of Cawdor. The present structure dates from the mid-fifteenth century and although some fourteenth-century stonework survives, no trace remains of the eleventh-century castle of Macbeth legend, which lay nearby.

A little closer to Auldearn, only 4 miles distant on the B9090 at Piperhill are the remains of RAF Brackla (Pathfinder 161–863515), established in 1941 as a Relief Landing Ground for RAF Dalcross, later becoming a satellite of RAF Kinloss. Over 2,500 RAF/WAAF personnel endured hard winters here. Towards the end of the war, the airfield was used for the storage and eventual breaking up of Halifax bombers. Anyone with the facilities and foresight to have preserved one of these cast-offs would have secured a priceless future collector's item. Little survives today, although the existence of a distillery off the southern perimeter road does provide an example of highly commendable post-war use of such a facility.

Further Information

Auldearn is situated on the A96, 2½ miles to the south-east of Nairn. The nearest railway station is in Nairn, which lies on the Inverness–Aberdeen line. There are connecting services to Glasgow and London Euston. A

The battlefield at Auldearn from the vantage point by Boath Dovecote. (National Trust for Scotland)

Bluebird bus service operates between Nairn and Auldearn, telephone 01224–212266 for details.

A free publication, *On the Move*, provides useful practical information including opening times and entry fees in respect of places mentioned in the Further Explorations section. Write or call Inverness Tourist Information Centre, Castle Wynd, Inverness IV2 3BJ on 01463–234353.

Ordnance Survey maps are Pathfinder 161 and Landranger 27. The battles fought by Montrose are not discussed as fully as one might wish in the standard battlefield guides. Inexplicably, Howard Green, in his *Guide to the Battlefields of Britain & Ireland* fails to mention any at all, while David Smurthwaite's *Complete Guide to the Battlefields of Britain* dismisses them in a few sentences. Similarly, Peter Young and John Adair in *From Hastings to Culloden* limit their coverage to three pages. It is left to Colonel H.C.B. Rogers in his *Battles and Generals of the Civil Wars 1642–1651* to give detailed accounts of Auldearn, Alford and Kilsyth. Martyn Bennett's *Traveller's Guide to the Battlefield of the English Civil War* contains an illustrated chapter on Montrose and *Walking & Exploring The Battlefields of Britain* by John Kinross has a section on Auldearn. As might be expected, the biographies of Montrose all cover the Battle of Auldearn. An outstanding study is Edward J. Cowan's *Montrose: For Covenant and King*. In terms of readability, John Buchan's *Montrose* has stood the test of time.

4
THE BATTLE OF KILSYTH
15 August 1645

Introduction

After Lieutenant-Colonel Hurry's failure to crush Montrose at the Battle of Auldearn, the commander-in-chief of the Army of the Covenant, General Baillie, found himself under pressure to step up the tempo of his campaign. This was more easily said than done for, having suffered successive defeats at the hands of the Royalists, the government troops were losing their appetite for the struggle.

In England, matters were swiftly coming to a head and on 14 June 1645, the Roundhead army won a decisive victory at Naseby in Northamptonshire. The engagement proved that possession of a strong contingent of horse could lose a battle as well as win one, for a dashing cavalry charge led by Prince Rupert resulted in his prolonged absence from the field. By the time he rallied his men, it was too late and Parliament had won both the day and the Civil War. Charles now gave further thought to the possibility of joining Montrose, a course of action which Prince Rupert felt would be disastrous and tantamount to abandoning his responsibilities. Goring's west country army was still intact and Oxford was still secure, but although Charles could still count on 4,000 cavalry and a few thousand infantry, the long march to Scotland through enemy-held territory would be fraught with danger.

While the king pondered, Montrose kept on the move, for procrastination was a luxury in which he could not afford to indulge. Marching north to Keith, he discovered Baillie who again refused to be drawn into battle. Montrose therefore withdrew to the south, hoping that the Covenanters would follow. Sure enough, Baillie abandoned his defensive position, encouraged perhaps by the knowledge that Alasdair MacDonald and much of his Irish contingent were absent. Montrose halted to the west of Alford, deploying his men on Gallowhill, overlooking the River Don and, in particular, a ford (on the site of the present-day Bridge of Alford) which Baillie, in pursuit, would have to cross.

The Royalists were drawn up in six ranks. On the right and left wings respectively were cavalry (in total, around 250) commanded by Lords Gordon and Aboyne. In between, stretching along Gallowhill, from left to right, were four infantry divisions, commanded by Colonel O'Kean (leading such of Alasdair MacDonald's Irish as were present), John Drummond of Balloch, Angus MacDonnell of Glengarry and Nathaniel Gordon. A reserve under Lord Napier remained in the rear.

Baillie reached the ford on 2 July 1645 and would have declined to fight again had it not been for the urging of his masters, the Committee of the Estates. Despite the absence of Alasdair MacDonald, Montrose was fielding roughly an equal number of infantry – about 2,000 – as Baillie although the latter could count on 500 cavalry. Once over the river, Baillie barely had time to deploy when Lord Gordon led a charge aimed at dispersing the cavalry of the Earl of Balcarres on the Covenanters' left flank. Balcarres withstood the initial onslaught but was overcome by the intervention of Nathaniel Gordon's infantry, which concentrated on hamstringing the enemy's horses. Once Balcarres was broken, Gordon was able to turn in on the infantry's left flank as it clashed, head on, with the Royalist foot. With the appearance of Aboyne's cavalry on his right, Baillie realized that there could be only one outcome. As his infantry fell back towards boggy ground bordering the Don, he and Balcarres with the surviving horse, quit the field.

According to Montrose, only four Royalists were killed, while Baillie lost almost his entire force. Realistically, several hundred Covenanters must have perished, with Royalist casualties limited to double figures. Among the Royalist dead was Lord Gordon, apparently killed during the pursuit, and furnishing an illustration of the dangers to a battle's victors of an over-zealous chase.

The Road to Kilsyth

Following his success at Alford, Montrose marched to Fordoun, near Laurencekirk, where he was rejoined by Alasdair MacDonald with 1,400 men. So strengthened, he pushed on to Perth, where the Scottish Parliament was due to meet on 24 July, in the hope of intimidating the Covenanters into submission. The difficulty was that without the cavalry of Aboyne, absent on a recruitment mission, he lacked the military muscle for the successful implementation of his plan. Baillie, who could still call on his cavalry, called Montrose's bluff by attacking his camp at Methven, 5 miles to the west of

A view over the battlefield of Kilsyth from the Hanoverian positions.

Perth. Forced to withdraw in some haste, the Royalists abandoned some camp followers, Irish and Highland women who were butchered in the heat of the pursuit.

At Dunkeld, Aboyne finally appeared with a mixed force of cavalry, dragoons and infantry, enabling Montrose to advance on Perth once more. This time, it was Baillie's turn to retreat, for he still needed to make good the infantry losses sustained at Alford. Assuming a defensive position near the Bridge of Earn, he awaited the Royalists' arrival but, with their customary wariness, both sides avoided a confrontation, with Montrose moving away to the south and Baillie continuing his search for reinforcements. On 13 August, having acquired an additional infantry brigade, Baillie set off on the Royalist trail, crossing Stirling Bridge and proceeding to Hollandbush farm, in the vicinity of Banknock, about 4 miles from Kilsyth and the Royalist camp, which lay in meadows, occupied today by a reservoir.

On the morning of 15 August, Baillie marched from Hollandbush to high ground immediately to the east of – and overlooking – the rebel camp. Although his position was advantageous, the intervening ground between Baillie and the Royalists was very uneven, offering little scope for manoeuvring infantry or, in particular, cavalry. Members of the Committee of the Estates, accompanying Baillie, considered that the high ground to the north of Montrose's camp might have potential. Baillie advised them that he saw little to be gained, fearing that the Royalists would probably occupy the high ground themselves, meeting any Covenanter attacking force with vigour.

As for Montrose, he may have been undecided whether to withdraw or to stand and fight. Many of his new recruits were untried and undisciplined but, bearing in mind his narrow escape from Methven and also his 100 per cent record of success to date, he resolved to give battle. Estimates of the size of his army as it stood on 15 August 1645 vary considerably. His total infantry strength may have been as little as 3,000 or as many as 5,000, while his horse, a mix of cavalry and dragoons was in the region of 500 to 600. Again, the nature of the Royalist deployment is unclear, but Lord Ogilvy may have occupied the right wing and Alasdair MacDonald certainly occupied the centre, with Nathaniel Gordon's horse and infantry on the left.

An even greater disparity exists between minimum and maximum estimates of Baillie's strength. In his impeccably researched booklet *The Battle of Kilsyth, 1645*, Stuart Reid gives a base figure of 3,000 infantry, as against the widely accepted number of 6,000. Similarly, while the Covenanters' horse is often generously estimated to have been 800 strong, Reid suggests a more modest 360, giving Montrose a clear numerical advantage. Although more recruits, led by the Earl of Lanark, were on the way, Baillie appears to have been satisfied that the troops he commanded were adequate for the job in hand. Given the punishment he had absorbed so far at the hands of the Royalists, he would not have risked another battle without being sure that he possessed some advantage over Montrose, and so one is inclined to accept a degree of numerical supremacy. His deployment, like that of the Royalists, is uncertain, but Balcarres' cavalry occupied the right wing, near Banton, alongside the Earl of Lauderdale's infantry, with Home's and perhaps Loudoun's regiments on the left – the extreme left of the line possibly occupying a spot between Craigs farm and the present-day disused railway line.

The Battle of Kilsyth

The first move seems to have been made by Baillie who bowed to the pressure of the Committee by despatching Major John Haldane with a party of musketeers to take the high ground to the north. Instead of acting as instructed, however, Haldane veered off to the left towards a number of cottages, surrounded by walled enclosures, which a number of Royalist Highlanders had been sent forward to occupy. The reason why Haldane disobeyed his orders is unknown. He may have feared that the Highlanders intended to attack him and felt it necessary to deal with the threat before proceeding further. No sooner had he engaged the enemy, however, than more Royalists, including Alasdair MacDonald, rushed to the aid of their allies. As Sir Charles Firth in his *Cromwell's Army* has pointed out, such skirmishing could easily develop into an unintended battle. In this instance, although a battle would have resulted regardless, both commanders were now committed to engaging prematurely.

Attempting to re-establish control, Baillie instituted an orderly general advance only to see Home break ranks and go to Haldane's aid. Initially, the ground which had become the centre of the action was not advantageous to either side, the stone walls restricting the effectiveness of Baillie's musketeers as well as destroying the impetus of Alasdair MacDonald's preferred all-out charge. While it may have suited Baillie to sacrifice Haldane, in the interests of his wider strategy, Home's intervention and the subsequent stalemate in the enclosure area now wrested the initiative away from him, placing the final outcome of the battle firmly in the lap of the gods.

Balcarres, meanwhile, still attempting to wheel round to the north had come under pressure from some of Gordon's Royalist cavalry. Again, neither side could force a breakthrough. First, the Royalists forged ahead, only to find themselves in danger of being cut off from their main body, and to be saved from extinction by the timely intervention of Aboyne. It was not until Montrose threw in the rest of his cavalry that Balcarres was finally overcome, thus enabling the Royalist horse to turn in on the Covenanters' infantry. Evidently, the success of the cavalry spurred Alasdair MacDonald into action, for his men now scaled the walls to resume their onslaught on Haldane and Home's. With Balcarres' cavalry in flight and MacDonald's Irish in full flow, Baillie's infantry caved in and took to its heels.

According to tradition, only a handful of Covenanters escaped with their lives. As with previous encounters, such as those of Auldearn and Alford, however, many lived to fight another day, somehow escaping the Irish who sought vengeance for the massacre of their women during the retreat from Methven Wood. The placename of Slaughter Howe, where Home's regiment was cut to pieces, bears witness to the barbarities perpetrated upon the vanquished. Haldane, who must have been in the thickest of the fighting, survived and was promoted.

Two days afterwards, the Royalists entered Glasgow, its citizens finding that they had nothing to fear from Alasdair MacDonald's clansmen, who had been expressly forbidden to pillage the city. A few, unable to restrain themselves, were executed and MacDonald began to wonder whether his usefulness to Montrose was at an end. Edinburgh escaped even more lightly, with only a troop of horse under Gordon and Napier being sent to take the surrender. Only Stirling held out, but this did not unduly worry Montrose who had set up court in Bothwell Palace to bask in the attention of Covenanters who came to pay their respects and to profess loyalty to the king.

The Aftermath

While Montrose was enjoying his moment of glory in the Scottish lowlands, events in England had moved on apace. On 10 July 1645, Goring's Royalist army in the west had been crushed at Langport, as a result of which the king finally made up his mind to join Montrose. Unfortunately, he got no further than Doncaster, where he was forced to turn back. Although worse news was to follow with Prince Rupert's surrender of Bristol on 11 September, Charles was nothing if not stubborn. He refused to accept the inevitable, continuing to entertain hopes that now that Scotland was subdued, Montrose would be able to join him and reproduce on English soil some of his remarkable victories against overwhelming odds. However, although Baillie's army was *hors de combat*, there remained in England Leven's far stronger and more battle-hardened army, and in response to Covenanter appeals, General Sir David Leslie hastened north, crossing the border on 6 September 1645, at the head of about 6,000 troops, including 5,000 cavalry.

Montrose, whom Charles had now appointed lieutenant-governor and captain-general of Scotland, must have hoped to lure Leslie into the Highlands, to be teased, wearied and crushed – to be dealt with, in short, in much the same way as Baillie. He had been promised some 2,000 men by Roxburgh and Home if he marched to the border country in person, an offer which, despite its attendant risks, he could not afford to ignore, for he was now in desperate need of reinforcements. Alasdair MacDonald was knighted by Montrose, yet he might well have preferred being accorded the privilege of looting Glasgow. Apart from this and his dislike of Montrose's new-found friends, he and his men had no wish to be drawn into a lowlands war, which might entail service in the border country – and even beyond – so he took his departure, leaving behind him some of the Irish. Aboyne was the next to go. Like MacDonald, he had to defend his own estates and, also like Alasdair, he felt slighted by the apparent preference of Montrose for the company of his fair weather supporters. Never strong, Montrose's army had now dwindled to an all-time low.

Commanding probably only 500 foot and a small troop of horse,

Montrose was counting heavily on the promises of Roxburgh and Home, but at Kelso he learned that they had thrown in their lot with Leslie. From Kelso, he marched to Jedburgh and from there to Selkirk, pitching camp about a mile to the west of the town, near the hamlet of Philliphaugh.

The following morning – 13 September – was foggy. Montrose, secure in the belief that Leslie was nowhere in the vicinity, had spent the night in Selkirk, to be awakened by the news that the canny general was, in fact, making preparations to attack the Royalist campsite. Proceeding to Philliphaugh with all speed, Montrose rallied his men, the remnants of the once invincible Irish brigade and 200 horse, deployed to the right of the infantry. That there was at least a little time to spare is evinced by the fact that a small body of Royalist musketeers had the opportunity to dig trenches. Yet, all too soon, the enemy was upon them. Approaching from the south-west, Leslie split his force into two groups, the main body attacking the Irish head on, while more divisions came on from the right. Miraculously, both Royalist infantry and horse weathered the first part of the storm before, as Baillie had foretold, they were crushed by sheer weight of numbers. Against his will, Montrose was led from the field, abandoning his loyal veterans to the wrath of the Covenanters. The Irish were all but annihilated, those who surrendered being butchered along with their women, children and camp followers, despite having been promised quarter.

Philliphaugh is generally recognized as the end of the road for the king's cause in Scotland, even though Montrose was not quite finished. A fortnight after the battle, he was to be found only 20 miles from Glasgow, at Buchanan Castle, with a new army of 1,500 men, although with winter approaching, Leslie refused to allow Montrose to entice him into another confrontation. Pleas for help to Alasdair MacDonald fell on deaf ears and reinforcements despatched from England by the king only got as far as Dumfries.

Disregarding these temporary setbacks, Montrose continued to recruit from the north throughout the winter months, so that by the spring of 1646, he could again field an army of up to 5,000. With the return to England of Leslie and the defection to the Royalist cause of Lieutenant-Colonel Hurry – the man Montrose had beaten at Auldearn – the future seemed a little brighter. Then came the devastating news that the king, hoping to turn the Covenanters against the English Parliament, had surrendered to the Scots army at Newark in Nottinghamshire. As part of the price for their cooperation, the Covenanters forced him to order Montrose to demobilize his army and go into exile. Montrose obeyed, and on 3 September 1646, he embarked from Stonehaven on a Norwegian vessel, bound for Bergen – thereby consolidating his reputation as one of the king's most loyal and most ill-used subjects.

The Walk

Distance: 4 miles (6.44 km)

The Colzium Lennox Estate on Stirling Road (the A803) is a good starting point, with ample car parking in the grounds (Pathfinder 404–732784) (Point A). Strike out eastwards along a track which brings one to the north-west corner of Banton Loch. Ignoring the tracks bordering the water, bear to the left and then to the right, into the trees. Continue to the end of Dam Wood and then pause to survey the scene.

At this point (Pathfinder 404–738788) (Point B) one is probably slightly forward of the Royalist left wing and the ground occupied by Gordon's cavalry. To the north, above Drum Burn, is Slaughter Howe, scene of the heaviest fighting while, to the north-east, to the left of the path up ahead is Auchinvalley (Pathfinder 404–742792) and Baillie could be forgiven for allowing himself to be persuaded that the Highlanders 'falling up the glen through the bushes' and occupying Auchinvalley may have had their own designs on the high ground to the north.

Continue toward Auchinvalley, noting, as one enters the next field, that the path changes course from outside to inside the boundary. After passing Auchinvalley, the track continues upward towards Wester Auchinrivoch. An additional grassy path branches off to the right in the direction of the industrial site on Mill Road (Pathfinder 404–746790). At some stage in the past, it must have been a negotiable route, but towards the industrial site (once a mill and now a builder's yard) it becomes very boggy, the 'stepping stones' referred to on the map proving hopelessly inadequate. In any case, there is no easy exit onto Mill Road.

So, brushing aside the prospect of a short-cut, press on to Wester Auchinrivoch (Pathfinder 404–745795) (Point C), which lay in the path of Baillie's outflanking march. Having reached what is, in effect, a minor crossroads, turn to the right and follow the track down to the village of Banton (Pathfinder 404–750793). At the crossroads, turn right into Mill Road which, further down towards the A803, becomes Banton Road. The builder's yard marks the approximate centre-right position of the Hanoverian army, stretching away to right and left of the road.

Carry on into Banton Road, crossing over the dismantled railway. One is tempted to branch off here, but the track, on low-lying land, is enclosed and sometimes waterlogged. The final field on the left as one approaches the A803 is known as 'Bullet Knowes' suggesting, perhaps, that this is one of the areas in which bullets were frequently dug up in later years. Bodies were buried far and wide, with bones being excavated as far east as Auchinloch

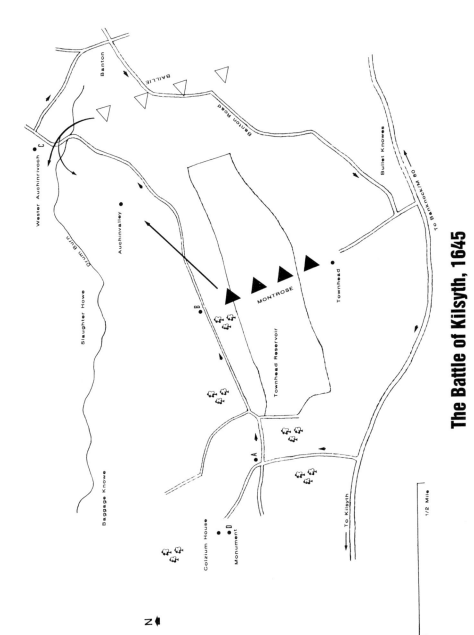

The Battle of Kilsyth, 1645

N

Baggage Knowe

Slaughter Howe

Drum Burn

Wester Auchinrivoch • C

Banton

BAILLIE

Banton Road

Bullet Knowes

To Banknock/M 80

Auchinvalley •

• B

MONTROSE

Townhead Reservoir

Townhead •

• A

Colzium House •

Monument • D

To Kilsyth

1/2 Mile

(Pathfinder 404–767788). At the junction, turn right onto the A803 and follow the excellent footpath back to Colzium.

The estate itself is worth a little exploration, in part because it contains a modern monument to the battle. Unlike the customary phallic symbol, this is fashioned in the shape of a curling stone (Point D). It is located, not very prominently, on the remains of the terraced gardens in front of the house, which has a local history museum.

At 4 miles, the walk is comparatively short and, of course, much of the battlefield itself is under water. Banton Loch is a man-made reservoir, but the casual visitor who might think that some interesting comparatively recent 'finds' must have been made on the occasion of its construction, would be mistaken, for the land was flooded in the eighteenth century. Even then, antiquarians decried the obliteration of the site, pointing out that until that time it had been possible to follow the course of the battle fairly accurately. Two hundred years later, it is possible to view the change of land use in a different light, with Kilsyth constituting one of the few Scottish battlefields to retain an entirely open aspect.

Further Explorations

One of the most interesting features of the surrounding landscape with a military connection is to be located immediately to the south of the old Forth & Clyde Canal, in the course followed by the Antonine Wall (Pathfinder 404–735768). During the AD 120s Hadrian's Wall had been established along a line stretching from the River Tyne to the Solway Firth. Less than twenty years later, work began on the construction of the Antonine Wall, as part of a plan to subjugate the lowland tribes. This new boundary ran a distance of 36½ miles from Bridgeness on the Firth of Forth to Old Kilpatrick on the River Clyde, and comprised a stone-based turf rampart with a ditch, 40 ft wide and 12 ft deep, to the north with a road, the Military Way, to the south.

Nineteen heavily garrisoned forts, about 2 miles apart, were built along the wall, while signalling platforms, to facilitate beacon fires, were sited to the rear. At Croy Hill (Pathfinder 404–734765), the site of one of the forts may be viewed, along with two beacon platforms – which were built in pairs – and a stretch of the wall ditch. A little to the west is the highest fort, at Bar Hill (Pathfinder 404–704759), with the foundations of the headquarters building and the bath-houses.

In a sense, the Antonine Wall provided a second line of defence as Hadrian's Wall was still occupied. It certainly proved to be a strain on resources and was twice abandoned when the garrisons, tying up a total of some 6,000–7,000 men, were needed to help quell uprisings further south. Finally, *c.* AD 185, it was abandoned altogether.

The area is not particularly rich in castles, a notable exception being the fifteenth-century Castle Carey (Pathfinder 404–787775), with a square keep five storeys in height. From 1640, the castle was in the ownership of the Baillie family and is reputedly haunted by the ghost of General William Baillie. After being partially destroyed in 1715 during the Jacobite wars, it was acquired by the Dundas family who undertook much restoration work. To the north are the earthworks of one of the Antonine Wall's stone forts (Pathfinder 404–790783) and it is said that the site was ravaged for materials in Castle Carey's construction. A glance at Ordnance Survey Pathfinder 404 indicates further vandalism when, in the 1840s, the Edinburgh–Glasgow railway line was driven through the site.

A Roman altar may be found to the east of Cumbernauld Village (Pathfinder 404–755762) with the site of a Roman camp – obliterated by an industrial estate – to the north (Pathfinder 404–778775).

According to many popular guide books, the town of Kilsyth itself has little to commend it, some gazetteers failing to make mention of it at all. However, a more than cursory examination reveals that it once had its own castle – the fifteenth-century Kilsyth Castle, home of the Livingstone family. Captured by Cromwell during his 1650–1 campaign, only fragments have survived (Pathfinder 404–717786). Finally, a visit to the town's cemetery (Pathfinder 404–715772), once the site of Kilsyth Kirk, is rewarding in so far as it contains a tombstone indicating that this was the burial place of Jean, Lady Dundee, the widow of James Graham of Claverhouse, Viscount Dundee, who was killed at the Battle of Killiecrankie (see p. 86). It is said that when her lead coffin was accidentally opened in 1795, the bodies of Jean and her infant son, embalmed before burial, were found to be perfectly preserved.

Further Information

Kilsyth lies on the A803 and is best approached via the M80/A80, at the point where the motorway ends and the trunk road begins (Pathfinder 404–788793). The Colzium Estate, starting point for the suggested walk, is about 3½ miles to the west. English motorists may be unfamiliar with the design of motorways in Scotland. In England, the tendency is for traffic to keep to the left, so that vehicles aiming for destinations off to the right filter to the left and cross the carriageway by means of an overpass. In Scotland, one often finds oneself veering over to slip-roads on the right – an interesting example, perhaps, of a way in which Scotland still has more in common with continental Europe than with her neighbour south of the border.

The nearest railway station is Croy, on the Glasgow–Falkirk line (telephone: 0345–212282 for details). From Croy, a pleasant walk of just over one mile leads one to the Colzium Estate. Alternatively, a Midland Bluebird bus runs hourly between Glasgow and Falkirk (telephone: 01324–613777).

Maps covering the area are Pathfinder 404 and Landranger 64. The *Ordnance Survey Street Atlas of Glasgow and West Central Scotland* also covers Kilsyth, but not to a sufficiently large scale to render it an adequate substitute for Pathfinder 404. In terms of further reading, the same problems apply to Kilsyth as to Auldearn (see pp. 40–1). Colonel H.C.B. Rogers's *Battles & Generals of the Civil Wars 1642–1651)* contains an illustrated account of the battle, while Edward J. Cowan's *Montrose: For Covenant and King* has a full chapter on the battle and the events leading up to it. Stuart Reid's booklet *The Battle of Kilsyth, 1645*, published by the Partizan Press in their English Civil Wargames series, is essential reading.

5
THE BATTLE OF DUNBAR
4 September 1650

Introduction

With the surrender of Charles I and the end of what is properly termed the First English Civil War, the victorious English Parliament had no further use for the Scots. As the king had first courted and then, when it suited his purpose, ditched Montrose, so Parliament now disregarded the obligations imposed upon it by the Solemn League and Covenant. Desiring only to wash its hands of the Earl of Leven's once indispensable Scottish army, the House of Commons engineered its dismissal with a down payment of £200,000 – a sum which secured both Leven's withdrawal and possession of the king, who was handed over to English Commissioners at Newcastle.

Had Charles appended his signature to the Covenant, agreeing to establish Presbyterianism, he would have secured the support of the Scots, and his failure to do so might, at first, be interpreted as an honourable course of action. Perhaps he thought he had more to gain by exploiting the growing differences between Parliament and the New Model Army. Fear of a military dictatorship did lead to a resurgence in popular support for the monarchy, and if Charles had bided his time, events might yet have turned in his favour. But in Scotland, too, opinion was divided – between those who wanted no compromise and others who were prepared to bargain, on the basis that a few faltering steps on the road to Presbyterianism were better than none at all.

On 11 November 1647, Charles escaped from custody to take refuge at Carisbrooke Castle on the Isle of Wight, a move which gave him sufficient freedom to resume negotiations with the Scots. These resulted in a contract known as the 'Engagement', with terms which provided for a Scottish invasion of England and the king's restoration to power in return for his agreement to establish Presbyterianism for a trial period of three years. When the Scottish Estates next met, it was the 'Engagers' who held sway, demanding the king's freedom and the fulfilment of the Covenant and, for good measure, the demobilization of the New Model Army.

With no prospect of the English Parliament acceding to any of these requirements, the Scots formed another army almost 10,000 strong. On 8 July, under the command of the Duke of Hamilton, it crossed the border and marched into Carlisle, where it was joined by Sir Marmaduke Langdale and a further 2,000 men. The invasion came at a bad time for Parliament, with Royalist insurrections breaking out all over the country. Sir Thomas Fairfax, commander-in-chief of the New Model Army, was tied up in the south-east, while his second in command, Cromwell, was trying to restore order in South Wales. With only 5,000 men under Major-General John Lambert to spare, these were difficult days for the Parliamentary cause.

Fortunately, Hamilton's army progressed only painfully slowly, giving Cromwell time to mop up in Wales before marching north to join Lambert at Wetherby on 12 August. Having gathered additional support, Hamilton's army may have numbered as many as 20,000, which, as it marched south, became strung out over many miles, the cavalry in the van arriving at Wigan while the rearguard was still at Preston. Cromwell, with only 8,600 men, chose to attack the latter, so cutting off Hamilton's line of retreat. On 17 August 1648, in an action which owed much, initially, to the personal leadership of Lambert who fought, pike in hand, at the head of the infantry, Hamilton's rearguard was broken. Hamilton himself hastened to Wigan to muster his cavalry. Learning that something was amiss, Lieutenant-General John Middleton, commanding the horse, had already taken the decision to turn back, and during the night of the 17–18 August, the two groups passed each other and Middleton managed to run into the enemy. Doubling back, he joined forces with Hamilton at Wigan and the remains of the half-starved, rain-sodden army set off for Warrington, with a view to making good defensive use of the River Mersey. Under continuous attack, all the fighting spirit left the grand army, the infantry surrendering in droves, so that by the time the Scots reached Warrington, only a scant few hundred remained to fight. Hamilton, with the cavalry, made good his escape, moving further into England in ever more despairing attempts to win support. On 26 August, he was taken prisoner at Uttoxeter, his surrender being taken, fittingly, by Lambert.

With Hamilton's defeat, the Covenanters formed a small army of 6,000 and advanced on Edinburgh to take over the reins of power. With Argyll at its head, the new government at once reached an understanding with the English Parliament, agreeing to discourage any remaining Royalist sentiment. Although it had not been their intention, this was taken to mean that they had no further interest in the future of the king, who lost his head on 30 January 1649. Less than a week later, the Scots recognized the Prince of Wales as Charles II, King of Scotland.

The Road to Dunbar

Unrealistically, the Prince of Wales was also proclaimed King of Great Britain, France and Ireland. With the New Model Army in control and the prince in exile, it seemed that Charles II would rule in name only, but he was, nonetheless, asked to subscribe to the Solemn League and Covenant. While willing to tolerate Presbyterianism in Scotland, however, he refused to commit England and Ireland without Parliamentary consent. It was a tactful response, geared to appeal to moderates of all parties.

Another condition pressed upon Charles by the Covenanters was the destruction of the Marquis of Montrose, now living in Brussels. Montrose had never relinquished his hopes of returning to Scotland to continue his fight for the Royalist cause and, having been thrown to the wolves by the father, he would shortly be led to the slaughter by the son. Having nothing to lose by encouraging Montrose, Charles appointed him lieutenant-governor and captain-general of all the royal forces in Scotland, with authority to mount a recruitment drive in norther Europe. With Montrose thus engaged on his behalf, Charles resumed negotiations with the Covenanters, an act which, in itself, did little to assist Montrose in his endeavours.

By the autumn of 1649, Montrose had succeeded in securing support barely sufficient to equip an advance party of 180 men under the Earl of Kinnoul, which was despatched to the Orkneys. The earl fell ill and died shortly after landing, and the new earl, with more supplies, sailed in January 1650, followed by Montrose himself towards the end of February. Upon his arrival, he received a letter – together with the Order of the Garter – from Charles, instructing him to proceed as planned, on the understanding that if agreement with the Covenanters should be reached, 'we will, with our uttermost care, so provide for the honour and interest of yourself, and of all that shall engage with you, as shall let the whole world see the high esteem we have of you'.

At the beginning of April, with a force of 1,600 men – which included his old adversary Sir John Hurry – Montrose crossed the Pentland Firth to the mainland. His intended advance to Inverness was hampered by the heavy cannon in his train and also by his desire to gather support on the way, so that by 25 April, he had got no further than the Kyle of Sutherland, spending the next two days in camp near Culrain, waiting for expected support from the Monroes and Rosses.

David Leslie, commanding the Covenanters' army, had marched north, via Inverness, to Tain, from where the Earl of Sutherland continued north, across the Dornoch Firth, while Colonel Strachan, the commander at

Major-General John Lambert, believed by some
to be the architect of Cromwell's victory at
Dunbar. (Mansell Collection)

Inverness, marched along to Kyle to confront the Royalists. In the afternoon
of 27 April, Strachan, his strength swelled by the Monroes and Rosses who
had thrown in their lot with him, approached the Royalist camp. In order to
surprise the camp, Strachan kept most of his men hidden, sending forward
only a single troop of horse. Believing that this small force was all he had to
face, Montrose deployed his men on open, level ground. As soon as they
were in position, Strachan produced his cavalry to put the untried
Orcadians to flight. Although the abandoned mercenaries gave a good
account of themselves, they were eventually overrun. As Montrose took to
his heels, how he must have wished for Alasdair MacDonald and his Irish
regulars, and for the cavalry of Gordon and Aboyne. But those days were
long gone.

Four days later, he was taken at Ardvreck Castle and handed over to his
enemies. Dressed in rags and an object of derision, he was strapped onto a
poor Highland pony, and taken to Edinburgh, to be hanged, drawn and
quartered, his head to be mounted on the Tolbooth at Edinburgh and a limb
each on the gates of Aberdeen, Stirling, Glasgow and Perth. The sentence
was carried out on 21 May 1650. A month afterwards, Charles landed at
Garmouth, near Elgin, having appended his signature to the Solemn League
and Covenant.

★

Fearing an invasion, the English Parliament decided to take the initiative before Royalists in England could rally to the cause. Fairfax, who disapproved of the idea, resigned his appointment as commander-in-chief of the New Model Army, providing the ambitious Cromwell with the opportunity to take over. The new commander-in-chief, who probably viewed the forthcoming campaign as a means of consolidating his position, wasted no time in getting underway, and on 28 June 1650, he marched out of London. On July 22, with 16,000 men, he crossed the border, intending to drive straight for Edinburgh.

The Scots, who had not been idle, had assembled an army of about 23,000, a figure which could have been much greater but for the influence of the Presbyterian clerics, who insisted on the dismissal of all veteran cavaliers and Engagers. As the New Model approached Edinburgh – with Lambert in the vanguard – it found Leven and David Leslie effectively blocking any assault on the city. On 29 July, an attempt to breach the defensive line was beaten off and the over-confident English, lacking both supplies and shelter, passed a miserable night in the rain. Forced to retreat, with Lambert now commanding the rearguard, they soon had Scots swarming all over them. It was left to Lambert to beat them off, in the process of which he was wounded. It is significant that while he recuperated, Cromwell made no attempt to resume hostilities.

A second march on the capital met with no more success than the first, leading to another retreat with Leslie, once again, harassing the rearguard. On 30 August, with an army reduced through sickness to only 12,000 men, Cromwell fell back to Dunbar, only to find himself outflanked by the wily Leslie who took up a position to the south of the town, on Doon Hill, thereby blocking the road to Berwick.

The Battle of Dunbar

Leslie hoped to force the New Model to fight without further delay, but although Cromwell's line of retreat to Berwick might be cut off, he could still depend on succour from the sea, via Dunbar. Therefore, he decided to dig in, leaving the Scots with no alternative but to relinquish their hilltop position. The rigours of a winter siege, with the possible eventuality of a relief force taking him in the rear was not to Leslie's liking, so on 2 September, he moved forward with a view to launching an all-out assault on the following day.

Watching the descent from Doon Hill, Lambert noticed that while the movement of Leslie's cavalry on the left wing was hampered by the Spott

Burn, level ground, offering potential for a New Model flanking manoeuvre, opened out to Leslie's right. A surprise attack on the exposed right wing might just carry the day. It was Lambert's idea, but Cromwell later claimed it as his own.

During the night, while the Covenanters sought shelter, Lambert deployed his men. General George Monck would command the infantry in the centre. To Monck's right, would be artillery and a limited force of cavalry, with cavalry on the left wing being commanded by Major General Charles Fleetwood and Lambert himself. To the left rear, would be Cromwell, taking responsibility for executing the planned flanking manoeuvre on Leslie's right, together with the infantry brigades of Colonels Overton and Pride.

The English guns opened fire at about 4.00 a.m. and the attack began. The Scots, who cannot have been completely unaware of the enemy's activity, appear to have responded quickly. Such was their numerical superiority that they were able to hold Monck's assault. Lambert's initial charge on the Royalist right came to grief for the same reason. Then, with the perfect timing necessary to the success of a set-piece manoeuvre, Overton's infantry pressed forward to bolster Monck, while Cromwell's cavalry pulled out to the far left of Lambert. As in the course of so many battles, the final outcome hung in the balance. Monck pressed forward once more and Cromwell, striking at Leslie's right flank seemed, momentarily, to be held, but the wholehearted commitment of Pride's accompanying infantry proved too much for the Scots. Lambert, also veering further to his left, charged again and Leslie's right flank broke. According to contemporary accounts, the results were both spectacular and decisive as the Covenanters recoiled along their line 'for three-quarters of a mile together'.

By full light, the battle was over. Immediately afterwards – so it was claimed – the victors downed weapons to sing the 117th Psalm chosen, perhaps, because, comprising only two verses, it is the shortest, thus facilitating the bloody pursuit to follow. For several miles, the Scots were pursued across country as they fled to Haddington in the east and towards Berwick to the south. The number of dead would have increased considerably during this period, though probably not to the extent of the 3,000 estimated by Cromwell. In a despatch to the Speaker of the House of Commons, he claimed that his own losses did not exceed twenty men – a statement at which even his most ardent supporters have expressed amazement. Several thousand prisoners were taken. Marched to Durham, these wretched survivors went unfed for a week and many died en route.

The English Parliament later arranged for a campaign medal to be distributed to the New Model officers and men. It was proposed that one side should bear an engraving of Cromwell's head. Although, initially, Cromwell averred that an engraving of the New Model Army would be more fitting, he was easily persuaded to change his mind. As far as commendations were concerned, the commander-in-chief remained conveniently reticent, airily proclaiming that the modesty of men, 'heroes-all', precluded anyone being singled out for special praise – especially, he might have added, the man responsible for the victory: John Lambert.

The Aftermath

While Cromwell the general may have had his rivals in terms of ability, Cromwell the politician was possessed of a shrewdness which was second to none. He knew that while Dunbar had broken the power of the Kirk – at least for the moment – it had also provided the king with greater freedom of action. With the Covenanters subdued, Charles, crowned at Scone on 1 January 1651, was now able to forge an alliance with both the moderates and veteran Royalists. Leslie's cavalry had survived, to form the nucleus of another army, and so a lasting peace was still far from being secured.

Cromwell was also intent on courting the Scots, combining reasoned argument with the power of the sword, in both of which activities, Lambert took a leading role. In the wake of Dunbar, Edinburgh and then Leith were occupied, forcing Leslie to retire, as many had done before him, into the stronghold of Stirling, and it was Lambert who probed for weaknesses in Leslie's defences. At length, in a desperate attempt to force Leslie's hand, Cromwell decided to move his army across the Firth of Forth, so threatening his own supply lines and driving a wedge between the Royalists and their supply lines to the north.

On 17 July 1651, Colonel Overton with 1,600 men crossed the Forth at Queensferry and quickly took control of the headland below Inverkeithing. In response, Leslie sent 3,600 men under Sir John Brown to keep them bottled up. Had not Lambert, on his own initiative, reinforced Overton, it is likely that the expeditionary force would have been overrun. Fortunately for Lambert, while his additional 3,000 men were being disembarked, Brown, following orders, remained immobile.

Apparently undecided as to how to act for the best, Brown dithered, first allowing himself to be drawn into limited action by skirmishing parties sent out by Lambert, and then retreating to high ground to the west of Inverkeithing. He may have been playing for time for, as Lambert discovered, Royalist reinforcements were on the way. Therefore, on the afternoon of 20 July – a Sunday – Lambert grasped the nettle by advancing on Brown's position. In the centre, Overton commanded the infantry, with Colonel Lydcot commanding six troops of horse on the left wing and Colonel Okey leading a greater concentration of horse on the right. The

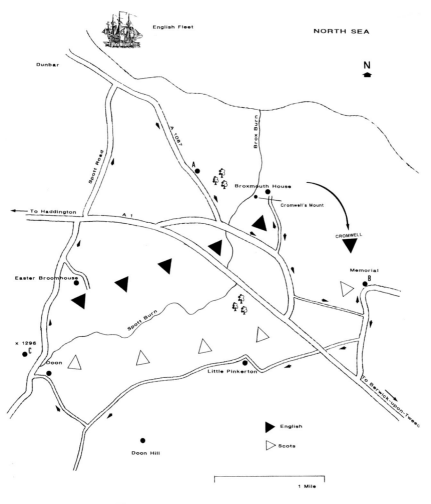

The Battle of Dunbar, 1650

Scots were ready for them and, as they pushed steadily uphill, Brown unleashed his lancers who scattered Lydcot's cavalry with ease. As demonstrated on many occasions, however, the impetus of a lancers' charge could carry them too far, as it did this time, giving Lambert the opportunity to cut off their retreat and attack them in the rear. This manoeuvre being successfully accomplished, Lambert continued his advance. Unwilling to risk a second counter-charge, Brown remained immobile. By the time the New Model infantry reached Brown's lines, their weariness seemed not to show for, in addition to sweeping the Scots aside, they were able to mount a devastating pursuit which resulted in the death or capture of all but a few hundred of the enemy, Brown himself being mortally wounded.

Meanwhile, Leslie and Cromwell continued to stalk each other, Leslie moving back and forth between Stirling and Torwood, about 6 miles to the south. Lambert's victory broke the stalemate, Cromwell deciding that the best course of action would be to link up with him and march directly on Perth, which he did, Perth capitulating on 2 August. Two days before, Leslie, with Charles in tow, had left Stirling to make a dash for the border, crossing into England on 6 August 1651. Whether Cromwell had anticipated such a move is a moot point. He may well have gambled on Leslie staying put – a course of action which the latter would have taken but for pressure exerted on him by a monarch who was anxious to claim the other half of his realm. Cromwell's critics suggest that he was caught unawares by Leslie's action, while apologists argue that the march to Perth was all part of a master plan to allow the Scots to invade. The truth of the matter is that after a year's campaigning, with no conclusion in sight, Cromwell was at his wits' end – a fact which is made clear in his letter of 4 August to the Speaker of the House of Commons: ' . . . if he [Leslie] goes for England, being some few days' march before us, it will trouble some men's thoughts . . . ' – a statement which would suggest that he had no idea whether Leslie intended to make for the border. Even if the worst happened, it was worth the risk, simply to draw the Scots out into the open. In the event, it was the Royalists who ran all the risks, staking all on a single throw of the dice.

The Walk

Distance: 10 miles (16.10 km)

An old section of the A1087, (Pathfinder 409–691788) bordering the Broxmouth Estate, to the east of Dunbar, serves both as a car-parking spot and a starting point for the walk (Point A). Proceed in a south-easterly direction, hugging the estate walls, to join the A1087. In so doing, one is walking the ground on which the bulk of the English army was initially deployed. On reaching the main entrance to the eighteenth-century estate (Pathfinder 409–698770), enter and follow the road to view Cromwell's Mount (Pathfinder 409–695776), the vantage point from which Cromwell and Lambert observed the disposition of Leslie's army. Return to the entrance and continue to follow the A1087 towards its junction with the A1.

Immediately beyond the railway line is a footpath off to the left, leading to the Blue Circle cement works. On reaching the complex, take the minor road over the bridge to reach the battlefield monument (Pathfinder 409–705768) (Point B), with an inscription by Thomas Carlyle. Such is the nature of the landscape that it is easy to pass it by. The Great North Road once ran through the gate to the right of the monument and on by Broxmouth to Dunbar. Quarrying gradually led to its disappearance so that today even the connecting footpath depicted on Pathfinder 409–699768 has been obliterated. However, the open country enables one to follow Cromwell's outflanking manoeuvre on a course which took him in a wide sweep from the rear of Broxmouth House to surprise the Scottish right wing, deployed on ground now occupied by the monument.

Return to the bridge and continue walking up the road running through the cement works to a track which leads off to the right. This minor road once led directly to Little Pinkerton, but in order to reach the hamlet, one has to cross the A1, which dissects the track. Although care has to be exercised, the A1 at this point comprises a single carriageway so that it can be negotiated without too much difficulty. Walk through Little Pinkerton, following the track out to the left, in the direction of Doon Hill, which dominates the local landscape. Leslie's infantry was drawn up immediately below the hamlet. His men must have passed but a poor night, foraging for shelter from the wind and the rain. Continue following the track, in a steady ascent of Doon Hill until a track branches off to the right, in a sharp descent towards Doon and the position occupied by the Scottish left wing. Follow the track around to the left to emerge onto the Spott–Dunbar road.

Turn to the right to cross over Spott Burn. It can be seen that Leslie's left wing, with the Spott Burn to the front and Doon Hill to its rear, had precious little room for manoeuvrability. In some ways, this is quite a significant little area for, looming up on the left is the site of an earlier Battle of Dunbar (Pathfinder 409–675762) (Point C). This encounter, a preliminary round in the Wars of Independence, took place in 1296, between Edward I's forces under the Earl of Surrey and John Balliol's Scottish nobles, resulting in a victory for the English.

Continue walking, to approach Easter Broomhouse on the right. English dragoons were deployed between Easter Broomhouse and Spott Burn, to the rear of the artillery and in a line stretching away towards Broxmouth. A little further along, this road makes a staggered junction with the A1 which, again, may be crossed with care. Continue through the trading estate and under the railway bridge onto Spott Road. At the junction, turn right into Queen's Road and continue along the A1087 back to the starting point.

Further Explorations

In addition to the features described during the walk, the locality has many other associations of a military nature. Perhaps its proximity to the Great North Road has rendered this inevitable. For example, Dunbar Castle (Pathfinder 409–678794) was once one of Scotland's most important border fortresses. Such was its ruinous state in the early years of the present century that when the celebrated travel writer H.V. Morton asked for directions, he received the reply: 'Man, ye're looking at it.'[1] Certainly, its history seems to be one continuous story of demolition, the Norman castle having been slighted as early as 1488. After some rebuilding, it fell into disuse in the late sixteenth century, to be demolished a second time in 1567. The castle's finest hour occurred in 1339 during the Wars of Independence, when it withstood a six-week siege with 'Black Agnes', Countess of March and Dunbar, holding out against the Earl of Salisbury's investing force until relief arrived by sea. On the opposite side of the harbour – construction work on which (1842) reduced the castle still further – are the remains of an eighteenth-century gun battery (Pathfinder 409–682794), designed to discourage coastal raids by pirates such as the American, John Paul Jones.

The town of Dunbar – created a Royal Burgh in 1370 – was razed to the ground by the English in 1544 and again in 1548. Not until the eighteenth century did it recover its former prosperity, only to lose it again in the twentieth with the decline of the fishing industry and of the coastal shipping trade in grain and potatoes. The parish church (Pathfinder 409–682786) has its roots in the 7th century, although it was rebuilt during 1818–21 and then again in 1987–92 after being gutted by fire. In thoughtfully landscaped grounds off West Port (Pathfinder 409–678788) are the remains of a thirteenth-century Trinitarian Priory.

To the south-west of Doon Hill is the hamlet of Spott (Pathfinder 409–672755), allegedly the location of the last witchcraft trial in the

---

1 With the harbour area much redeveloped since Morton's day, Dunbar Castle is now readily discernible.

The battlefield memorial at Dunbar. Thomas Carlyle's inscription has been worn away, and the memorial is a sad feature of the landscape, poised between a quarry and a cement works. Doon Hill is in the background.

lowlands. The victim, one Marion Lille, was the last of a long line of witches burned at the 'Witches' Stone' (Pathfinder 409–669752). A little further south, towards Spott Mill, is 'The Chesters', site of an Iron Age hill fort (Pathfinder 409–660739). Although worn away by centuries of farming activity, it is still an imposing sight.

To the east of Dunbar is Innerwick and Innerwick Castle (Pathfinder 409–735737). Owned by a branch of the Hamiltons, it suffered – like the town of Dunbar – at the hands of the Tudors. In 1548, the Master of Hamilton and eight companions tried to defend it against the English. All died in the attempt, and the castle was slighted. The incident is of interest as an example of the countless minor affrays which comprised a military campaign. At nearby Thornton (Pathfinder 409–740734), another castle fell to the English at the same time but, unlike Innerwick, Thornton Castle was not rebuilt.

If travelling up to Dunbar from the south via the A1, one should take the opportunity to visit Dunglass (Pathfinder 409–767718), an area which promises some splendid walking. Dunglass Castle, held by the Earls of Dunbar and, later, the Home family, has long since ceased to exist, although the present-day mansion was built on its foundations. In the grounds is the fourteenth-century estate church which survived an eighteenth-century attempt to convert it into a stable. Another interesting site is depicted on OS Pathfinder 409 as 'French Camp' (763717), a hill fort which was actually constructed by the English in 1548.

Further Information

Dunbar is one of the most accessible Scottish battlefields, straddling the A1, to the south east of the town of Dunbar. The starting point for the walk, near Broxmouth Gardens, is on the A1087, the A1's access road for Dunbar. Dunbar is on the main East Coast railway line linking London (King's Cross) and Aberdeen. Oddly, it is not included within the National Express coach network.

Ordnance Survey maps are Pathfinder 409 and Landranger 67. Unfortunately, they cannot be depended upon – Pathfinder 409 depicting a path running through a quarry. Even the *Ordnance Survey Street Atlas for Edinburgh & East Central Scotland*, published in 1995, does not include significant additions to the footpath network.

The *East Lothian Holiday Guide*, available from the Tourist Information Centre, 143 High Street, Dunbar (telephone 01368–863353) provides useful information for visitors to the locality. An additional booklet, *East Lothian Visitor Attractions and Activities*, makes no mention of the Battle of Dunbar.

Many of the classic texts on battlefields are limited to sites south of the border. Thus, the pioneering surveys of nineteenth-century writers such as Richard Brooke's *Visits to Fields of Battle in England*, and C.R.B. Barrett's *Battles and Battlefields in England*, are mute on Dunbar. Even twentieth-century surveys, such as A.H. Burne's *Battlefields of England*, as its title implies, include nothing further north than Flodden Field. Colonel H.C.B. Roger's *Battles and Generals of the Civil Wars 1642–1651* has a chapter on Dunbar, as does Peter Young and John Adair's *From Hastings to Culloden*. In addition, C.H. Firth's *Cromwell's Army* contains some stimulating observations as to Cromwell's conduct of the battle – Firth firmly believing that the strategy which won the battle was Cromwell's.

6
THE BATTLE OF DRUMCLOG
1 June 1679

Introduction

The defeat of Charles Stuart's army of Scots at Worcester on 3 September 1651 ushered in a welcome period of stability for a country rent asunder by civil war for nine years. His escape also spared the English Parliament the embarrassment of having to decide his fate.

From 1653, until his death on 3 September 1658, Cromwell 'reigned' as Lord Protector. Behaving as a conqueror towards the vanquished, he guaranteed freedom of worship in Scotland, but otherwise left the Scots in no doubt that their country would be treated in much the same way as an English county, with a limited number of seats in a projected joint Parliament. Although the years of the Protectorship are sometimes recognized as prosperous ones, there were many Scots, Royalists at heart, who would have preferred equality and not a few who still hankered after freedom.

Nothwithstanding all they tried to do for him, Charles entertained a sneering disregard for the Scots, professing that he would rather be hanged than return to Scotland. Of course, this did not stop him from sending others to agitate on his behalf – notably in 1654 when a Royalist force commanded by General Middleton was broken at Dalnaspidal.

In 1660, an England unable to fill the void left by Cromwell's demise, invited Charles to return in peace. Having successfully disposed of absolutism, it seems extraordinary that she should seek to re-establish the institution, particularly as Charles refused to bury the hatchet. Certainly, the principle of government by the consent of Parliament did not extend to Scotland, which was to be ruled by Commissioners, the first of whom was Middleton.

Heading the company of scapegoats whose executions were intended to purge Scotland of its late Cromwellian sympathies was the Marquis of

Argyll – the man who had crowned Charles at Scone. His final words on the scaffold were those of an unrepentant Covenanter and with him died, symbolically, the Solemn League. Yet, although the Scots might be prepared to modify their expectations in terms of the spread of Presbyterianism in England, Charles had no intention of tolerating rampant Presbyterianism in Scotland, insisting that it was 'no religion for a gentleman'. Nothing less than a return to episcopacy would do.

Such a policy was bound to lead to a confrontation between the newly consecrated bishops and the old ministers, and matters came to a head when Middleton tried to compel the ministers to apply for collation. In the face of overwhelming opposition, Middleton was recalled, to be replaced by the Earl of Rothes, who continued in the same vein, although with a little more discretion. Nonetheless, in November 1666, a rising among the peasantry in Dumfries culminated in the capture of Sir James Turner, commander of the small government force in the area. Although the insurrection was soon put down – with the customary quota of executions and transportations – Rothes was now recalled and the Earl of Lauderdale, confidante of the king, 'ruled' in his stead.

Although many non-conformist ministers grudgingly agreed to toe the new, relatively conciliatory, line pedalled by Lauderdale and returned to the fold, there remained a hardcore of extremists who preferred to roam the countryside, presiding over open-air services known as conventicles. Lauderdale countered in 1671 by making conventicle preaching a capital offence. The great fear of the government was that the conventicles might be used as a tool for the promotion of political unrest – as they were with armed 'congregations', several hundreds strong, roaming the hills. In practice, the law could not be enforced and so Lauderdale took the next most effective step by exacting heavy fines on landowners who were, it was argued, responsible for the actions of their tenants. With sections of both peasantry and landowners now suffering at the hands of the government, rebellion became inevitable.

The Road to Drumclog

The first major act of rebellion was the murder of Archbishop Sharp who had risen to prominence as a negotiator in the aftermath of the English Civil War. As both Archbishop of St Andrews and a Privy Councillor, Sharp had to balance political expediency against his wish for an independent church in Scotland – a skill at which he had proved adept.

On 3 May 1679, the sixty-year-old Sharp, accompanied by his daughter, was travelling by coach to St Andrews. The journey from Edinburgh was nearing the end as the travellers approached the village of Strathkiness, only 3 miles from their destination, when it became apparent that they were being followed by a group of hostile horsemen. The Archbishop's guard, consisting of only two armed servants, were easily dealt with and, when the coach had been brought to a halt, the bandits – as they appeared to be – forced an unwilling Sharp out of the coach and cut him to pieces. After ransacking the luggage, they rode off, leaving Sharp's daughter, Isabel, unharmed.

The Privy Council offered a reward of 10,000 marks for information leading to the arrest of the culprits, who, nine in number, were soon identified. The ringleaders, John Balfour and David Hackston, both lairds, seem to have mistaken Sharp for a lesser official against whom they bore a grudge, but few tears were shed for the archbishop whose dual role rendered him universally unpopular. Having already survived one attempt on his life, it is surprising that he ventured on a journey without a more substantial escort. Much was made of the fact that his valuables were ignored, as opposed to his papers, which Balfour carried away.

While the government was keen to use the incident as an excuse to crack down on the conventicles, its fears were not unfounded, for the opposition was also intent upon exploiting the situation. Foremost among the latter was Sir Robert Hamilton, an eccentric extremist who considered that the use of violence was justified in the achievement of his aims. On 25 May, Sharp's assassins, who had managed to elude the dragnet, joined forces with Hamilton at Strathaven, moving on to Glasgow where, with the help of sympathizers – including the town clerk – they compiled a list of grievances. Four days later, with eighty horsemen, they rode into Rutherglen and presided over a conventicle in the market square, at the conclusion of which papers representing the hated anti-Presbyterian Acts of Parliament were burned.

Such government troops as existed to enforce the laws in Scotland were always overstretched. In Glasgow, the Earl of Ross commanded a garrison of around 240 men. At the time of the Rutherglen incident, 20 miles away, at Falkirk, Captain John Graham of Claverhouse, a 31-year-old officer of dragoons, was making plans for joining Ross with a view to challenging a conventicle which he had heard was to take place on Kilbride Moor, near Glasgow, the following week. En route to Glasgow, he learned of the treasonable activities at Rutherglen and sent a detachment of troopers to deal with the problem.

On 30 May, Graham arrived in Glasgow, remaining there until the following day when he left for Rutherglen. From there, he pressed on to Hamilton, where he made a few minor arrests, discovering in the process that the very next day, a conventicle would take place to the south of Strathaven, in the vicinity of Loudoun Hill. To break up conventicles wherever he found them was Graham's duty but, instead of having his meagre force augmented at Glasgow, he had actually left a company with Ross, so that when he arrived in Strathaven on Sunday 1 June, he had with him only 120 men.

The Battle of Drumclog

After breakfasting at the Slate Inn in Strathaven, and having received confirmation of the rumoured conventicle, Graham continued at a steady pace towards Loudoun Hill. The event was, in fact, being held on the nearby Harelea Hill and, as he approached from the high ground to the north, Graham may have heard songs of praise and perhaps even the words of its fiery preacher, James Douglas, borne aloft on the still morning air.

According to some sources, the meeting numbered some eight or nine thousand souls, a generous estimate considering the barrenness of the location. Whatever the actual total, the worshippers appear to have been warned of Graham's advance for, by the time of his arrival on the scene, most of the women and children had been moved to safety. Unfortunately for Graham, the armed guard was quite intimidating, consisting of Sir Robert Hamilton with 60 men and Balfour and his followers. In addition, perhaps 200 poorly armed but determined able-bodied members of the congregation stood ready to defend their right to worship.

Therefore, the situation facing Graham did not match his expectations. Instead of a peaceful meeting which would disperse hurriedly, leaving him free to pick up the ringleaders at leisure, he was faced with organized resistance. Although his men were professionals, he himself had seen no major action and, with his force outnumbered by at least two to one, his response required careful consideration.

From the shelter of Loudoun and Harelea, the Covenanters had advanced to take up a position on the high ground occupied today by Stobieside, leaving Graham to ponder the options open to him: fight or withdraw. In order to advance on the rebels (for rebels he considered them to be) he would have to negotiate some very boggy ground. Having sent a rider back to Glasgow with a request for reinforcements, he demanded the surrender of the insurgents. When this was not forthcoming, he sent in a skirmishing party but, instead of scattering as he had hoped, the rebels formed an advance party of their own – the two sides exchanging one or two volleys of musket fire before the rebel skirmishers withdrew.

What was Graham to do now? Reinforcements would be long in coming and it began to look as though the rebel resolve might not weather a

The Battle of Drumclog. An example of the way in which artists have invariably – and usually misleadingly – depicted Scottish battles as being fought within a landscape of almost primeval proportions. (National Army Museum)

sufficient show of force. So, Graham ordered a general advance. He must have foreseen that the advantage he had over the enemy – his cavalry – would be rendered largely ineffective by the nature of the terrain, but he gambled on his positive action throwing the rebels into confusion. He could not have guessed that the rebels, throwing caution to the winds, would respond by launching a fast and furious assault on their own.

As Graham himself later reported, the amateur rebel infantry began its advance, guided perhaps by local men among their number who knew how to negotiate the mire. The dragoons stood their ground, but their fire cannot have been confined to disciplined volleys, for the rebels seem to have experienced little difficulty in coming to grips with them. Moreover, William Cleland, the minor poet, leading the rebel infantry, managed to outflank the government force on its left wing. In the confused melée, Graham's horse was wounded by a pitchfork-wielding rebel to an extent which caused it to bolt, carrying its rider from the field. Despite the severity of the wound which Graham claimed it had sustained, the animal managed to carry him three miles to Hillhead, where he commandeered his trumpeter's horse to take him on to Glasgow.

Those under his command who remained on the battlefield stood little chance. Deducing that Graham had fled voluntarily, the rank and file followed suit, although many were surrounded and butchered, while several more fell in the pursuit. At Strathaven, the hostile inhabitants seem to have been on the alert, for they attempted to block the road, forcing the fleeing survivors to fight their way through. Darkness had fallen by the time they reached Glasgow, accompanied by Ross's reinforcements, whom they had met on the road only 6 miles out.

The Aftermath

As far as casualties were concerned, Graham may have lost about ten dead, with many more wounded, while rebel losses, minimized by the victors, may have stood at three to six dead. The importance of the encounter, however, lay in the confidence which the victors now had in their abilities as a fighting force. Having defeated regular troops they felt capable of marching straight on to Glasgow, which they reached the following morning, after a night's rest at Hamilton.

Divided into two parties, the rebels charged into the town at about 11.00 a.m., to be met by concentrated musket fire from Ross's men, sheltering behind hastily erected barricades. Unable to make further progress, the rebels withdrew, and one can only speculate what might have happened had not the Earl of Linlithgow lost his nerve and ordered the evacuation of the garrison. As soon as Ross had left, Hamilton and the rebels moved in – a turn of events which suggested that the Covenanters were now very much in the driving seat. In this respect, the rebellion, which might have been contained at the embryonic stage, can be viewed as the product of an irresolute administration.

The king's reaction was to send the Duke of Monmouth to Scotland to take charge. Monmouth, who had seen action on the continent, arrived in Edinburgh to take command of Linlithgow's army on 18 June. The lowland militia were hastily assembled and just three days later, on 21 June, the combined government force, including Graham and the veterans of Drumclog, was advancing on Glasgow. The Covenanters, on the other hand, had failed to use their time so expediently. In the wake of their success, their numbers had swelled to around 6,000 but, as expected, they had fallen to arguing among themselves, their days spent in tedious religous discussion.

The final reckoning occurred 10 miles to the south-east of Glasgow, at Bothwell, where a substantial bridge spanned the River Clyde. The rebel army, still locked in heated theological debate, camped on the west bank, awaiting Monmouth who had been sighted approaching from the east. Some efforts were made to settle the dispute by peaceful means, but talks broke down with Monmouth's insistence that the rebels lay down their arms unconditionally.

Hostilities commenced on the morning of 22 June with an artillery duel at close quarters – Monmouth's four pieces against the rebels' one. At first, the latter's luck held, for Monmouth's gunners were driven back. Lacking the leadership necessary to exploit this advantage, the rebels remained on their side of the river, a forward party holding the bridge with the help of a barricade. Such was their lack of foresight that scant regard had been paid to the matter of ammunition, so that the rebel muskets soon fell silent and Monmouth's gunners were able to regain their positions. Their fire, coupled with that of the musketeers, forced the rebels onto the defensive, giving the government cavalry that chance for which they had been waiting. Their ammunition all but spent, the rebels watched as Monmouth's troops swarmed across the bridge. The rebel left wing was the first to give way, infantry and horse alike buckling under the pressure of increasingly accurate cannon fire. Panic spread along the line and the entire rebel host took to its heels.

In the aftermath, Monmouth, who would have preferred to exercise a degree of clemency, must have lost control, for the pursuit was particularly vicious – some of the roughest treatment being dispensed by Graham in revenge for Drumclog. Hamilton, together with Balfour and Hackston, escaped, leaving 800 dead behind them. A further 1,200 prisoners were treated with exemplary cruelty, countless deaths resulting from ill treatment, while others were transported to Barbados. Strangely enough, Graham came out of the affair very well and, a month later, he accompanied Linlithgow to the court of Charles II, where, in an audience with the sovereign, he did his level best to scupper Monmouth's moderate views, arguing that a ruthless policy was the only realistic option. The king obliged.

The Walk

Distance: 10 miles (16.10 km)

Begin at Drumclog Memorial Kirk (Pathfinder 457–640389) (Point A), which stands at the junction of the A71 and the Torfoot road (the B745). Built in 1912, and replacing an earlier structure, the kirk was named in remembrance of the Battle of Drumclog. A service commemorating the battle is still held annually on the first Sunday in June.

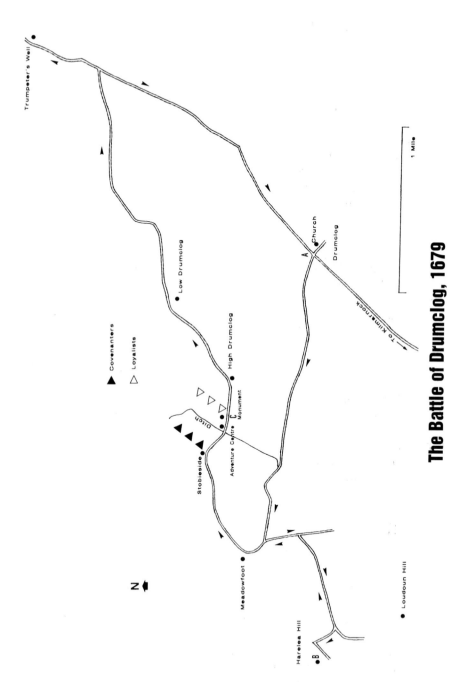

The Battle of Drumclog, 1679

Covenanters
Loyalists

N

1 Mile

Trumpeter's Well
Low Drumclog
High Drumclog
Church
Drumclog
To Kilmarnock
Monument
Ditch
Adventure Centre
Stobieside
Meadowfoot
Harelea Hill
Loudoun Hill

A
B
C

Leaving the kirk, cross the A71 (with care) and take the minor road towards Meadowfoot. In the seventeenth century, much of the land hereabouts was marshy but the drainage systems which have since been imposed upon the landscape now make it difficult to visualize the boggy terrain which existed at the time of the battle. Walk past Drumclog Cottage, as far as the junction, and turn left. Looming up ahead – and visible for miles around – is Loudoun Hill (Pathfinder 457–408379). Loudoun is the site of an encounter which took place on 10 May 1307, between Robert the Bruce and the English Earl of Pembroke, and is regarded as a turning point in the king's fortunes. Heavily outnumbered, Robert's men dug trenches to counter enemy cavalry charges. Hurling themselves recklessly onto the Scottish pikes, the English horsemen were beaten off and, with them, the entire army.

Instead of walking on to Loudoun, turn to the right, towards Winkingfield. Follow the road around past the settlement, to arrive at Harelea Hill (Pathfinder 457–401388) (Point B), where the Covenanters were holding their service on the morning of the battle. Now walk back to join the Meadowfoot road and continue on to Stobieside (Pathfinder 457–622398) where the Covenanter force drew up – 'a most advantagious ground to which there was no coming but through mosses and lakes', as Graham noted in a subsequent report to the Earl of Linlithgow.

The road dips towards the Drumclog Adventure Centre, on the east wall of which is a memorial to the Covenanter casualties. A little further along is the battlefield monument (Pathfinder 457–625396) (Point C) near the position taken up by Graham. Apparently, undergrowth screened the boggy terrain between the two groups, so that Graham remained unaware of it. The hill occupied by Stobieside is, indeed, 'advantagious' while, even without any undergrowth to obscure the view, the descent from the monument to the foot of the hill is deceptively gradual. One may imagine how gingerly the dragoons approached the 'stank brae', seeking a firm footing for the mounts on what was, to them, unfamiliar ground.

After exploring this limited area, continue along the road, following, in reverse, via High Drumclog, the route taken by Graham on his march from Strathaven. Eventually, the road terminates at the A71.

A busy road, the A71 does not constitute a pleasurable walk. However, it is worth a walk of half a mile towards Strathaven in order to view the 'Trumpeter's Well' (Pathfinder 457–661417). It was here that a handful of Graham's men, including the trumpeter, unsuccessfully tried to surrender to their pursuers, before being cut down. Opposite is Hillhead, where Graham's badly wounded horse collapsed, and one is left to ponder the truth of subsequent claims that he commandeered the trumpeter's mount, thereby sealing the unfortunate man's fate. Certainly, Graham did well to flee, for one of his officers – also named Graham – was fearfully mangled by

The battlefield of Drumclog, looking from the memorial towards Stobieside. Drumclog
Adventure Centre is on the left.

the Covenanter mob in the mistaken belief that he was Graham of
Claverhouse.

After viewing the well, proceed (with care) back along the A71 to the
starting point at Drumclog Memorial Kirk.

Further Explorations

At first sight, Strathaven (Pathfinder 445–703445), like many of the smaller
Scottish towns, is disappointing, particularly for anyone passing through on
the busy, uninviting A71. In this case, first acquaintance is misleading, for
there is much to interest the military historian.

To begin with, Strathaven has a castle (Pathfinder 445–705444). Built in
the mid-fifteenth century by Andrew Stewart, Lord Avondale, it was bought
by the Marquis of Hamilton in 1611, remaining in the hands of the family
until 1912, when it was given to the people of Strathaven. In fact, they had
already taken it, having for years helped themselves to the stones for use in

the construction of their own houses. Militarily, it came to the fore during the seventeenth century, in particular after the Restoration, when it was garrisoned with a view to combatting local Covenanter sympathies. In the adjacent graveyard is a memorial to two Covenanters, John Barrie and William Patterson, numbered among those who were executed for refusing to take the oath of allegiance.

Across from the castle is the Army Cadet Hall, standing on the site of the Slate Inn, where Dundee breakfasted before the Battle of Drumclog. The inn, which later became known as The Claverhouse, survived until 1932 when it was demolished – indicating that Strathaven's interest in the preservation of its heritage is of comparatively recent origin.[1] The cemetery (Pathfinder 445–705447) contains stones commemorating William Dingwall, killed at Drumclog, and another commemorating Barrie and Patterson.

The John Hastie Museum in Threestanes Road (Pathfinder 445–699447) features the Battle of Drumclog among its numerous displays. Its most interesting item is the Avondale Covenanters' flag, woven in Strathaven and bearing the motto 'Avondale for Religion, Covenant, King and Country.' It is believed that Sir Robert Hamilton carried the flag at Drumclog, using it to rally the Covenanters.

Ten miles to the north of Strathaven is Bothwell (Landranger 64–7157), scene of the defeat of the Drumclog Covenanters by the Duke of Monmouth. Industrial development continues to encroach upon the battlefield, but the action may still easily be envisaged. A monument to the encounter is situated on the Bothwell side of the bridge. Bothwell Castle (Landranger 64–6859) is one of the most renowned fortifications in Scotland. Founded in the late thirteenth century by the Moray family, it soon fell to the English, in whose hands it remained for just over a year, being retaken by the Scots, following a fourteen-month siege, in 1299. In 1301, it fell again to the English, thanks to Edward I having commissioned an enormous siege engine known as a belfry – a portable wooden tower with a platform at the top. The medieval equivalent of the modern abnormal load, it was hauled on a two-day journey from Glasgow, along a specially constructed road. After Bannockburn, the castle reverted to Scottish control, although the English were to occupy it again in 1336. When liberated by its owner, Sir Andrew Moray, it was slighted – Moray demolishing his own home in accordance with the scorched earth policy instituted by King Robert I. In later life Bothwell had a succession of owners, including both the Black and the Red Douglases, who were

---

1 The old jail was demolished as recently as 1963.

responsible for much restoration work. The most interesting part of the castle is the surviving portion of the great thirteenth-century keep. Originally 65 feet in diameter, with walls fifteen feet thick, it was surrounded by a deep moat, beyond which the land fell precipitously to the river.

Opposite the castle, on the south bank of the River Clyde, are the remains of the Augustinian Blantyre Priory (Landranger 64–6859) – a house of God and a house of war separated only by a narrow stretch of water.

Further Information

Motorists will approach Drumclog on the A71, a busy road connecting the M74 with the west coast, at Irvine. The Torfoot turning, by the church, is deceptively sharp and the road narrow. The most direct route to the Adventure Centre and the battlefield is via Hallburn (Pathfinder 445–655408).

Strathaven once had its own railway station, but the line connecting it with Glasgow has long since closed. The course of the line, which ran roughly parallel with the A71, can easily be followed (Pathfinder 445–675425). The nearest stations for today's rail traveller are Hamilton and East Kilbride. A bus service linking East Kilbride and Hamilton and operated by Henderson Travel (telephone 01698–710102) takes in Strathaven.

Strathaven has an excellent Tourist Information Centre housed in the Town Mill Arts Centre in Stonehouse Road (telephone 01357–29650), with free leaflets providing historical background on the area's Covenanter association, and also information on the Battle of Drumclog itself.

Two Ordnance Survey Pathfinders are required: Nos. 445 and 457. The Landranger map is No. 71. Although the Battle of Drumclog was of significance to the hopes of the Covenanters, and played an important part in the shaping of John Graham's future career, it is generally regarded as little more than a skirmish due to the small number of participants. Hence, few battlefield texts take the trouble to discuss the encounter. It is mentioned briefly in David Smurthwaite's *Complete Guide to the Battlefields of Britain*, but one has to look to Graham's biographers for detailed accounts – notably *For King & Conscience: John Graham of Claverhouse, Viscount Dundee* by Magnus Linklater and Christian Hesketh.

7
THE BATTLE OF KILLIECRANKIE
27 July 1689

Introduction

In 1681, James, Duke of York, was appointed Lord High Commissioner for Scotland in place of Lauderdale who had fallen from grace as a result of the minor rebellion of 1679. Brother to Charles II, James had survived a period of banishment following his suspected involvement in a Catholic plot to assassinate the king. His move to Scotland was seen by some as an extension of his exile.

The new commissioner arrived just in time to preside over the introduction of the 'Test Act', which required all office holders to swear an oath of loyalty to the Church and state. With the exception of the royal family, all extremists, Catholics and Covenanters together, would be effectively barred from public office. Assisting James in the implementation of one of the most unpopular pieces of legislation of all time was the veteran of the Battle of Drumclog, John Graham of Claverhouse, who had attached himself to the duke as a means of winning preferment. The Earl of Argyll refused to take the oath and, tried for treason, was compelled to flee to Holland. Others who refused had to resign their public offices, and Graham benefitted in this respect by having conferred upon him several forfeited appointments.

Graham's commander-in-chief, General Sir Thomas Dalyell, remembering the débâcle at Drumclog, had little time for his subordinate. However, sporadic fighting between government and Covenanters, in which Graham was often involved, continued in the south-west. In a phase of exceptional government brutality, known as the 'Killing Times' (1685–6), Graham allegedly played a key role in several barbarous incidents. While the most lurid details were certainly added years after the event, there can be no doubt that Graham carried out his duties somewhat over-zealously. While realizing that unrest resulted from the activities of a minority of extremists, he was quite prepared to hunt down and summarily execute unarmed

'Bonnie Dundee' or 'Bloody Clavers'? An early portrait of John Graham of Claverhouse, later Viscount Dundee – a man so supernaturally wicked, according to his enemies, that it took a silver bullet to kill him. (Scottish National Portrait Gallery)

individuals who refused to take the oath of allegiance, and it is to his activities in this period that Graham owed his sobriquet 'Bloody Clavers'.

It may be that Graham was seeking to assure the new king of his continued loyalty, for Charles II died in February 1685, to be succeeded by the Duke of York, who became James II of England and VII of Scotland. Immediately, James made it clear that there would be no let-up in the persecution of Covenanters and Graham, whose enemies had, from time to time, placed a strain on his friendly relations with his mentor, must have been anxious to press his suit at this most opportune time.

Thanks to the initial panic occasioned by the rebellion of May–July 1685, led by the Duke of Monmouth and the Earl of Argyll, Graham was raised to the rank of brigadier. In the event, the new brigadier was not called upon to exercise his military talents, for the rebellion came to nothing, Argyll failing to attract support in Scotland and Monmouth being defeated in England at the Battle of Sedgemoor.

James would have been well advised not to proceed with his master plan to convert his realm to Roman Catholicism, for the removal of barriers blocking the preferment of Catholics had to be presented within the context of toleration for all. That same policy which helped Catholics to high office in England also allowed the Presbyterians to regain lost ground in Scotland, at the expense of Episcopalianism, thus breaking the alliance between the monarchy and the Church, which Charles II had laboured so diligently to establish.

James had one daughter, Mary, who had married William of Orange in 1677, and now, ten years later, a group of leading English peers, led by the Earl of Shrewsbury, invited William and Mary to save their country from a return to Popery. On 5 November 1688 – a fitting date for a revolution – William landed at Torbay, with an army of invasion which included English and Scottish brigades in its number. Desperate to amass an army of his own, James called on every available soldier north of the border to march to his assistance – an order which included Graham, who was created Viscount Dundee & Lord Graham of Claverhouse. But the expected battle failed to materialize for James, in the face of a series of desertions – notably that of John Churchill, the future Duke of Marlborough – lost his nerve. Ordering his commander-in-chief, the Earl of Feversham, to demobilize, he sought to escape to France. Captured at his first attempt, he was permitted to succeed at the second.

Fortunately for Dundee (as John Graham of Claverhouse now became known), he had cultivated William many years before while serving under him in the war between Holland and France. It was even rumoured that he had saved William's life. Surely, then, Dundee's star would remain firmly in the ascendant?

The Road to Killiecrankie

During his relatively short lifetime, Viscount Dundee chose to commit two acts which were at variance with his overweening plans for self-advancement. One was his marriage into a family of Covenanters and the second, his lukewarm response to William's overtures of friendship. In February 1689, William and Mary accepted the throne of England while Dundee, with William's agreement, was permitted to return to Scotland.

The problem for many Scots – as well as English – lay in assessing the strength of William's position. In the end, a Scottish convention, preferring William's conciliatory approach as opposed to James's forthright demands, came down in his favour. Yet James still had supporters, both at home and abroad, who believed him to be the rightful king. An invasion backed by William's arch-enemy, Louis XIV, might well result in a victory for James, and some influential Scots, including Dundee, began to explore the possibilities for a Jacobite revival.

Perhaps Dundee dreamed of future greatness for, if he were to take the lead in a successful counter-revolution, then surely all Scotland would be his for the asking? Whatever his motives, he was touting for support at a very early stage, and planning to organize a rival convention at Stirling. His friend, Colin Lindsay, the Earl of Balcarres, could be counted upon as, he hoped, could the Duke of Gordon, Governor of Edinburgh Castle, together with the Marquis of Atholl and the Earl of Mar, Governor of Stirling Castle.

On 18 March 1689, leading a troop of his own men, Dundee left Edinburgh, but without Balcarres and Atholl who had both decided to remain behind. Gordon, already outlawed, appeared to be wavering and so, instead of making for Stirling Castle and the proposed Jacobite convention, Dundee headed for Dudhope Castle, his home. The irresolution of his comrades had rendered his own position untenable and, like Gordon, he became a fugitive from justice. On 11 April, William and Mary were proclaimed king and queen of Scotland and a few days later, Balcarres was thrown into prison. Dundee was on his own.

In fact, James, accompanied by a 3,000 strong French army, had landed in Ireland. Based in Dublin, he attracted enormous support. Instead of looking to an early invasion, however, he laid siege to Londonderry where he remained, tied down, for three precious months. Dundee was not to know this. Outlawed, he had nothing to lose by declaring for James and holding out until help came. On 16 April, therefore, he raised James's standard on Dundee Law, to the north of Dudhope, before riding off into the Highlands, to seek the support of the clans.

Dundee's activities throughout the next few months owed much to the strategy employed by Montrose, with whom Dundee has been compared. In this respect, Major-General MacKay, the commander-in-chief of William's army, was led a merry dance throughout the country, much as Baillie had been out-manoeuvred by Montrose forty-five years earlier. But Dundee also suffered from Montrose's main problem: a perennial shortage of manpower, rivalry between the clans and their view that plundering was an acceptable part of campaigning, making it doubly difficult for Dundee to maintain discipline. The Macdonalds of Keppoch, proficient cattle rustlers, were to prove especially rapacious. As for MacKay, from the outset, much of his infantry was engaged in a siege of Edinburgh Castle and, again, like Baillie before him, he did not wish to risk a major encounter until his army was up to strength.

Despite his caution, MacKay could hardly afford to give Dundee a free hand to recruit in the north, and followed him to Inverness. Here, Dundee would have made a stand, but for the departure of the MacDonalds, who were anxious to return home with their rustled cattle. With MacKay advancing laboriously from the east, via Elgin and Forres, Dundee therefore marched south by Blair Atholl and the Pass of Killiecrankie, to Perth where he executed a successful raid on the evening of 10–11 May. Although he acquired some horses, the real benefit lay in the kudos gained by having struck a blow at one of MacKay's bases. Unfortunately, an attempt on the city of Dundee the following day failed.

The viscount then turned his attention to the west, marching to Mucomir, at the southern tip of Loch Lochy, near Fort William, where he hoped to rendezvous with a substantial army from Ireland. It failed to materialize, although the MacDonalds of Keppoch did reappear, together with some Camerons and bands of warriors from several of the smaller clans. On 28 May, this ramshackle force moved north and two days later, attacked and burned Ruthven Castle. MacKay marched out from Inverness, but decided against giving battle. Outnumbered, he retreated, Dundee giving chase – a situation which was reversed yet again when the opportune arrival of reinforcements gave MacKay the upper hand once more. Occasionally, he came upon clansmen who had lagged behind the main column but, when cornered, they responded with such ferocity that the government troops were encouraged to maintain a respectable distance. Finally, on 14 June, Dundee arrived at Strone, a little to the south of Mucomir. Some clansmen drifted away, while others came in – each clan, like the Danes of old, anxious to take its fill of looting, Again, MacKay passed up an opportunity to fight. Arguing that he was in need of supplies, he withdrew to Inverness.

By 20 June, MacKay was on the move again, this time with the purpose of establishing a number of Highland garrisons – a strange idea which would put a further strain on his limited resources and which would succeed only in delaying the day of reckoning. On 12 July, he arrived in Edinburgh, to gain approval for his plans, and where he was cheered to find that the Duke of Gordon had, at last, surrendered the castle. The longer Dundee waited at base for his Irish reinforcements, the greater likelihood there was of his being isolated in the far west. In an effort to avoid this predicament, he resolved to consolidate a foothold in Atholl. Knowing that he could depend on the steward of Blair Castle, he instructed him to hold it in his name. The Marquis of Atholl having withdrawn from the contest, the castle was under the control of his son, Lord John Murray, at that time conveniently away in Edinburgh. On his return, Murray, whose loyalties had hitherto been divided, was thus reduced to laying siege to his own home.

By this time, Dundee was armed with an official commission from James, but when the promised army arrived, it comprised only 300 poorly provisioned tribesmen. All told, having less than 2,000 men at his command, Dundee decided to set out for Blair Castle, where he planned to hold a further rendezvous with such clansmen who had yet to come in. Unknown to Dundee, MacKay had also set his sights on Blair and on 22 July, he left Edinburgh with a view to joining Murray at the siege. With 4,000 men and siege engines, his progress was delayed sufficiently for Dundee to reach Blair ahead of him. At Dundee's approach, Murray withdrew, enabling the former, on 26 July, to march into the castle unopposed. MacKay, fuming at Murray's irresolution, stopped short at Dunkeld, where he spent the night, looking forward, no doubt, to the following day when he would surely bring this tiresome campaign to an end.

The Battle of Killiecrankie

On the morning of 27 July 1689, MacKay broke camp and set out on the road to Blair Castle. At Pitlochry, he was joined by a shamefaced Murray, before moving on towards Killiecrankie. At the Pass of Killiecrankie, he halted. Here, the thickly wooded ground rose sharply to the east. A better spot for an ambush could not be imagined, and MacKay scouted the area thoroughly before moving on. With some relief, he emerged into more open country, overlooked by the eminence of Creag Eallaich, where he halted once more.

Dundee had not made such an early start. Had he done so, he might well have caught MacKay in the pass. His route had taken him over high ground to the north, via Fenderbridge and Loch Moraig, from which point he followed the course of the Allt Chluain between Lude Hill and Creag Eallaich, in a descent towards Killiecrankie. His advance guard was spotted when MacKay's column was stretched out on the road below Urrard House. MacKay reacted quickly, but not speedily enough to stop Dundee deploying above him along the slopes of Creag Eallaich.

Having been beaten to the high ground, MacKay ordered his men to wheel to the right, to assume a position on fairly level land, on either side of Urrard House. His force of 3,500 men was deployed in a rather over-extended line due to his fear of being outflanked by the more mobile clansmen. On the extreme left of his line were Lieutenant-Colonel George Lauder's fusiliers, flanking the infantry brigades of Brigadier Bartold Balfour, Colonel George Ramsay and Viscount Kenmure. On the right wing were the three infantry brigades of the Earl of Leven, MacKay's own (commanded by his brother, James) and, on the extreme right, Colonel Ferdinand Hastings. In the centre, MacKay placed his modest artillery and, to the rear, his cavalry, 100 strong, under the command of Lord Belhaven. In sum total, if not a strong force, it was adequate for the task in hand.

If MacKay's line was over-extended, then Dundee's, comprising under 2,000 men, must have appeared positively skeletal. On the extreme right were the MacLeans of Duart, then the Irish contingent, commanded by Colonel Alexander Cannon and the MacDonalds of Clanranald, Glengarry and Glencoe, with the Grants of Glenmoriston and the Stewarts of Appin.

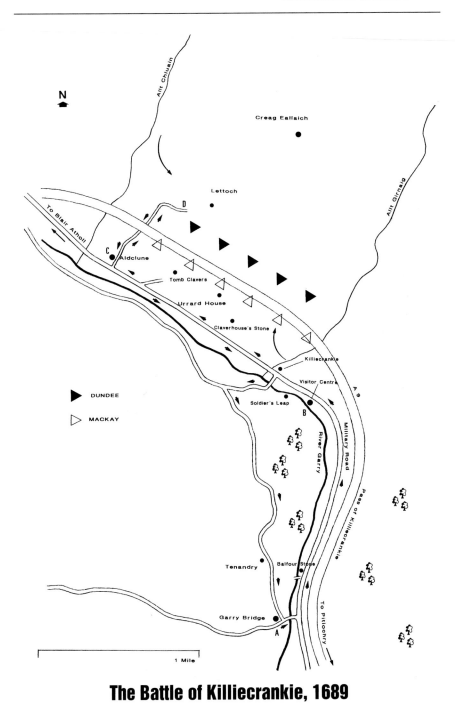

The Battle of Killiecrankie, 1689

On the left were the MacDonalds of Sleat, the MacLeans of Otter, the MacDonalds of Kintyre and the Camerons of Lochiel. In the centre, opposite MacKay's cavalry, were forty horse commanded by Sir William Wallace.

Remarkably, apart from a minor action in which a party of Cameronians sniping at the enemy left wing were driven off, the two armies remained immobile for the remainder of the day – MacKay's artillery proving useless. Not until 8.00 p.m. did Dundee order his men to charge. Although it seems that each was assigned a target, the vista presented to MacKay's men was one of a mass of ferocious savages bearing down upon them.

To their credit, the government troops remained outwardly calm, firing two or, at most, three volleys into the advancing clansmen. Although their ranks were thinned, the Highlanders came on, the first clash occurring on MacKay's right. As they struggled to fix bayonets – which had superseded the pike – James MacKay's infantry were overwhelmed. James himself was killed, although Dundee's entire right wing, from the MacDonalds of Seat to the Camerons, seems to have swept through the gap, in pursuit of his fleeing men, and some of Leven's who were carried along with them.

Before the battle, Dundee had been warned against placing himself in danger. Nevertheless, he, too, joined in the attack, with Wallace's cavalry at his heels. Suddenly, Wallace veered away to his left, leaving Dundee to proceed alone. When he realized what had happened, Dundee half-turned in the saddle, raising his left arm to beckon the cavalry forward. As he did so, a bullet struck him in the side and he fell from his horse.

On Dundee's right wing, the course of events mirrored that on the left, with the Highlanders absorbing punishing musket fire before tearing into the opposition with their broadswords. Balfour's brigade had collapsed immediately, his men outflanking their comrades in a dash for the pass, where many of them – along with James MacKay's infantry – were cut down by their pursuers.

In the centre ground, the fate of Kenmure's brigade was sealed when Belhaven's charging cavalry, in a manoeuvre similar to that of Wallace's horse – perhaps occasioned by the sight of marshland ahead of it – wheeled to its left, falling back on its own infantry. When Ramsay and Lauder gave way, and MacKay's left wing ceased to exist, the outcome was decided. Amazingly, Hastings's battalion and half of Leven's remained intact on the right, and MacKay managed to organize a fairly orderly retreat, across the River Garry, to safety under cover of the gathering darkness.

The pursuit, apart from the slaughter of the pass, was not so devastating as it might have been, many of the pursued owing their lives to the Highlanders' interest in MacKay's well-stocked supply train. Even so, MacKay's losses were heavy enough, with his dead estimated at anywhere between one and two thousand, and another 500 taken prisoner. The

Highlander dead numbered about 500 but included, as always, many of their leaders – a price they always paid for leading from the front. Most significantly for the Jacobite cause, however, Dundee himself lay dying on the battlefield.

The Aftermath

For a few days, with characteristic rapidity, wild rumours spread throughout the land to the effect that MacKay's army had been decimated and that the conquering Dundee was about to descend on the Lowlands. While it soon became apparent there was some truth in the first part, the administration experienced a sense of relief when news of Dundee's death filtered through, for the Jacobite cause in Scotland was now leaderless.

Dundee's body was laid to rest in the church at Blair Atholl, where it remained. The morning after the battle, far away in the dungeons of Edinburgh Castle, the Earl of Balcarres had a vision in which a weary, armour-clad Dundee, complete with the fatal wound in his side, appeared before him. Had Dundee's spirit returned to bid farewell to his friend or, perhaps, to chide him for his faint-heartedness? It is just one of many stories which comprise the Dundee legend.

As anticipated by his surviving followers, Dundee's death created a vacuum which could not be filled, and they would have been well advised to disperse to their homes. However, recruits to the cause – unaware of the situation – were still arriving at Blair Castle in response to his earlier call, so that within three weeks, a force of 5,000 men had assembled. Colonel Cannon, commander of the Irish brigade, oversaw some ineffectual forays, including a particularly disastrous raid on Perth, before clashing with the Earl of Angus's newly formed regiment in the small town of Dunkeld, mid-way between Perth and Pitlochry, on 21 August 1689.

By this time, Cannon's strength had dwindled to some 3,000 men, although they still outnumbered the defenders of Dunkeld, commanded by William Cleland, by three to one. Cleland, it will be remembered, had faced Dundee – as a rebel – at Drumclog. Now, ten years on, Dundee's men were the rebels. And as Dundee had lost his life in leading his men to victory at Killiecrankie, so Cleland, in turn, forfeited his own life at Dunkeld. The Highlanders' mode of warfare was little suited to the town's narrow streets, and they were mown down in their hundreds by disciplined volleys of musket fire. When Cannon eventually withdrew – claiming a victory – the '89 Jacobite rebellion was over.

While it is possible that Dundee could have capitalized on Killiecrankie, in the long term he would still have been hamstrung by his dependence on Highlanders whose preference was for short fighting seasons in which looting played a key role. And MacKay had learned valuable lessons from his defeat. The new bayonet fitted awkwardly into a musket's muzzle, which meant that, apart from the time factor involved in the process, a musket could not be fired once the bayonet had been fixed. MacKay, having ruefully noted the effects of this at Killiecrankie, devised a method of fixing a bayonet to the side of a musket. The time was coming when battles would be fought at a distance, the outcome to be decided by the strength of one's firepower, thereby rendering the Highlanders' mode of waging war redundant. MacKay also continued to lobby for a series of Highland forts, efforts leading, initially, to the establishment of Fort William and, ultimately, of Fort George at Inverness, Fort Augustus at the southern tip of Loch Ness, Ruthven Barracks at Kingussie and Bernera Barracks on Glenelg Bay off the Sound of Sleat.

Many of the Highlanders remained fiercely loyal to the memory of Dundee and all that he had stood for. On the other hand, it is almost needless to add that, even as Dundee fell, the Stuart for whom he sacrificed himself was planning to betray him.

The Walk

Distance: 6 miles (9.65 km)

Begin at Garry Bridge, immediately to the south of the Pass of Killiecrankie, on the B8079 (Pathfinder 294–912609) (Point A). From the bridge, follow in the footsteps of General MacKay's army by walking along Wade's Military Road, through the Pass of Killiecrankie. It must be borne in mind that this road was not constructed until 1728, and that before then the route comprised a narrow, muddy track. Until the comparatively recent introduction of the new A9, the pass was a potential death-trap for unwary pedestrians – as it was in MacKay's day, although for different reasons – and one must still keep a sharp lookout for the occasional careless motorist. However, the A9 construction necessitated the clearance of trees to the east of the old road, so that the aspect is now much more open.

Before reaching the hamlet of Killiecrankie, one arrives at the National Trust for Scotland's Visitor Centre (Pathfinder 294–917627) (Point B), which is mainly concerned with woodland management, although it does have welcome displays on the subject of the battle. Readily available leaflets

Tales of extraordinary athletic feats performed by escaping soldiers in the aftermath of battle are not uncommon. 'The Soldier's Leap' at Killiecrankie is, undoubtedly, the most celebrated of such legends. (The National Trust for Scotland)

will direct one to 'The Soldier's Leap' (Pathfinder 294–915626), scene of the best-known anecdote about the battle. According to the official version, a government soldier, Donald MacBean, was fleeing on horseback – with a Highlander in close pursuit – when he reached this spot. Dismounting, he clambered onto the angular rock and leapt a distance of 18 feet, to land safely on the other side. According to another version, as the escapee jumped, his pursuer slashed at his back, effecting a wound several inches in length. Later employed by General Wade in road building, he would often display his scar as proof of his story. The instructive aspect of the incident, of course, is that a single Highlander could instil such terror into a mounted and fully armed soldier that, rather than fall into his pursuer's clutches, the man would cast away his horse and his weapons, and make a death-defying leap across a gaping chasm.

Beyond Killiecrankie, the land begins to open out, and it was here, near the present-day Urrard House, that MacKay halted. Claverhouse's Stone (Pathfinder 294–908632) marks the position of the government baggage train. While Wade was building this stretch of road, he fell into conversation with a veteran of the battle who was firmly of the opinion that MacKay would have won if he had placed his supply train in front of his army as an enticement to Dundee's Highlanders.

Continue walking, past Urrard House, to Aldclune (Pathfinder 294–898637) (Point C). It was from here that MacKay's forward scouting party noticed a group of Highlanders making their way down from the high ground. From this initial sighting, only moments seem to have elapsed until Dundee's main force came into view.

Take the track which leads up, alongside the trees, towards Lettoch. The track crosses the A9, slightly forward of Mackay's final positions following the deftly executed manoeuvre in which the government force swung around to the north and advanced uphill to a point beyond Urrard House. At the other side of the A9, continue on, hugging the field boundary, until a point directly below Mains of Orchil is reached (Pathfinder 294–905641) (Point D). Dundee's army would have descended the lower slopes of Creag Eallaich immediately to one's rear.

As one looks down towards the A9, it will be noted that the two forces must have been very close to one another. And all through the afternoon, they remained immobile. Mackay did remark that the enemy was within musket range, and it appears likely that when the Highlanders finally charged, the government infantry could manage only two rather than three volleys before they were overrun.

Another monument, 'Tomb Clavers', supposedly marking the spot where Dundee fell, lies in a field between one's vantage point and Urrard House (Pathfinder 294–905636). According to a local tradition, Dundee was watering his horse at a spring when he was shot from a window of Urrard House. It does seem likely that MacKay would have concealed marksmen in the house and outbuildings, which the Highlanders themselves eventually occupied, but the tale tends to lose credibility with the claim that Dundee was carried from the field to expire in the Inn of Blair – which later became the home of the Blair estate factor – in the grounds of Blair Castle, for the viscount certainly died on the field of battle.

Retracing one's steps – along a route which would have placed one in the midst of the wild Highland charge which destroyed Balfour's lines – return to the B8079 and walk back, past Urrard House, towards Killiecrankie. On the left is a track leading up to the field (privately owned) containing 'Tomb Clavers'. Immediately beyond Allt Girnaig is a minor road bridging the railway line and the River Garry. Take this road for an attractive alternative route to Garry Bridge and the starting point. Keep bearing to the left, passing Tommacnell and Tenandry, with its small church. Before completion of the walk, one final monument may be viewed by taking the footpath by Garry Bridge. Walk down as far as the footbridge, cross over and, turning left, continue along the footpath as far as the Balfour Stone (Pathfinder 294–915613), the spot where Brigadier-General Balfour was killed, spurning offers of quarter.

Further Explorations

If approaching Killiecrankie from the south, one will have passed by Pitlochry (Landranger 52–9458), 4 miles away. This small town, which has built up a substantial tourist industry, developed from the adjoining village of Moulin. Often failing to warrant a mention in the guidebooks, Moulin should not be ignored by the discerning traveller. Remains of a castle, Black Castle (or Castle Dubb) may, for example, be seen nearby (Landranger 52–947589). Built about 1320 by Sir John Campbell, a nephew of Robert I, it occupied a strong position in the middle of a shallow lake. Moulin's church is Victorian although, allegedly, the site has been a place of worship since AD 490, when a church was established here by St Columba. Evidence of a much earlier civilization exists in the form of a standing stone (Landranger 52–943594) and stone circle (Landranger 52–935588).

Before reaching Pitlochry, the northbound traveller will also pass by Dunkeld (Landranger 52–0242), once the end of the road as far as communications with the interior were concerned. It was the construction of General Wade's military road linking Dunkeld with Inverness which opened up the country between the two settlements. In the sixth century, the Pictish King Conal built a monastery here for St Columba and, in so doing, established a long and celebrated ecclesiastical connection. The cathedral (Landranger 52–025426) dates from the twelfth century, although much of that which survives is fifteenth century in origin. It will be remembered that William Cleland lost his life here in the defence of the town after Killiecrankie. And it is Cleland who must be held responsible for the burning of old Dunkeld – an incongruous act for a poet to have committed. Several properties, built after the fire, have been restored through the efforts of the National Trust for Scotland.

Adjoining Dunkeld is Birnam (Landranger 52–03411) and Birnam Wood, referred to in *Macbeth*. One of the fancied locations for Macbeth's castle is Dunsinane Hill (Landranger 53–2131), but this would appear to be rather distant from Birnam Wood.

To the north of Killiecrankie is Blair Castle (Pathfinder 294–865663), which has not been included in an extension of the suggested walk, due to the fact that it would take the best part of a day's tour to do justice to the castle and grounds. The oldest part of the structure, Comyn's Tower, dates from 1269, when building began under the direction of David Strathbogie, Earl of Atholl. Its strategic position meant that it was the scene of military activity during the first five centuries of its life. Montrose turned it into a Royalist stronghold in 1644, while from 1652–60, it was garrisoned by General Monck's soldiers for the Protectorate. On the evening before the

Battle of Killiecrankie, it will be remembered, Viscount Dundee stayed there and it was Dundee's decision to challenge General MacKay's army, as opposed to settling for a holding action at Blair that won him the battle and cost him his life. After this, the castle was partially dismantled. Prince Charles Edward spent three nights here in September 1745, and the following spring, Lord George Murray unsuccessfully besieged Sir Alexander Agnew's Hanoverian garrison, in what was to be the last siege of a castle in the history of warfare in Britain. During the siege, over 200 red hot cannonballs were fired at the castle and, had not Murray been called away to Inverness and thence to Culloden, the defenders – so short of water that they had to cool the cannonballs in tubs of urine – would surely have had to submit. In 1844, Queen Victoria visited Blair and was sufficiently amused as to grant permission for the Dukes of Atholl to maintain a private army: the Atholl Highlanders.

Dundee, as already noted, was buried in St Bride's kirk in Old Blair (Pathfinder 294–868665) – Wade's military road makes uncharacteristic twists and turns to circumvent the River Tilt, crossing the watercourse at the Old Bridge of Tilt (Pathfinder 294–877665), and running by the church, before resuming a more direct course to Bruar.

Further Information

Potentially one of the most isolated of battlefields, Killiecrankie is very accessible – the Pass of Killiecrankie constituting as important a routeway today as it did 300 years ago. Although the new A9 trunk road cuts through the middle of the battlefields, the old 'low' road, following the route of General Wade's Military Road, was woefully inadequate for modern requirements and a potential death-trap for ramblers. Motorists approaching from the north should take the old A9 (the B8079) at Bruar (Pathfinder 294–822658). If approaching from the south, one should join the B8079 at Pitlochry. Car parking is available at Garry Bridge and the Visitor Centre.

Blair Atholl still has a mainline railway station, and it is possible to travel direct from London (King's Cross) to Blair Atholl, via Edinburgh. Trains also run from Glasgow. Details of coach services to Pitlochry can be obtained from National Express (telephone 0990–808080) and/or Scottish Citylink (telephone 0990–505050).

For up-to-date details of opening times and entry fees of the National Trust for Scotland Visitor Centre at Killiecrankie, call 01796–473233. The Perthshire Tourist Board, 45 High Street, Perth PH1 5TJ (telephone

01738–38353) will also supply useful visitor information. The future of Blair Castle is in some doubt following the recent (1996) death of the 10th Duke of Atholl, and it is hoped that Scotland's most visited privately owned home will continue to welcome visitors. For up-to-date visitor information, telephone 01796–481207.

Pathfinder 294 covers the area of the suggested walk, but Pathfinder 309 (Pitlochry) is also useful, together with Landranger 43.

Like the Marquis of Montrose, Viscount Dundee is quite neglected by military historians. In his case, the neglect is understandable because his career falls between the English Civil War and the later Jacobite rebellions. As with the Battle of Drumclog, one has to look to Dundee's biographers for detailed accounts of the Battle of Killiecrankie – notably Magnus Linklater and Christian Hesketh in *For King & Conscience: John Graham of Claverhouse, Viscount Dundee*, and Andrew Murray Scott in *Bonnie Dundee*. Scott is sketchy on Drumclog but gives an excellent account of the Killiecrankie campaign.

8
THE BATTLE OF SHERIFFMUIR
13 November 1715

Introduction

Although Jacobite unrest is usually referred to in terms of individual risings, most notably the '15 and the '45, the period between 1688 and 1745 was one of continual unrest. And for thirty years after Culloden, the Jacobite flame would be kept burning by the mere existence of Charles Edward Stuart, and occasionally kindled by French expansionist ambitions.

The years after Killiecrankie were particularly distressing ones for Scotland, ushering in one of the most harrowing periods in Scottish history. As the campaigning season of 1690 opened, an attempt was made to resurrect the rising of the previous year, but this belated effort collapsed almost immediately, with the defeat at Cromdale in Strath Spey on 1 May 1690, of a modest Jacobite force led by Major-General Thomas Buchan.

The fate of James VII was decided in Ireland. The mainland threat to William III's position now much reduced, the king sailed to Ireland in June 1690. At the head of a huge army of 36,000 men, including his own incomparable Dutch Guards, he routed James at the Battle of the Boyne. James fled back to France, leaving his Irish and French supporters to continue an increasingly static campaign, terminating in a series of sieges – punishing for both the besieged and the besiegers – at Limerick, Cork and Kinsale.

With Ireland subdued, William hoped to mop up any lingering resentment in Scotland with a mixture of bribery and coercion. It was hoped that the distribution of £12,000 among the Highland chieftains would help to reduce the number of clans still holding out, but for those who could not be bought, the Earl of Breadalbane and Sir John Dalrymple, Master of Stair – both Campbells – acting for the king, announced a deadline of 1 January 1692 for the chiefs to take the Oath of Allegiance. Even then, the demand had to be watered down to the extent of allowing the Highlanders to seek

James's permission. Surprisingly, this was forthcoming, although not until late in December 1691, and one chief, Maclan of the MacDonalds of Glencoe, did not manage to take the oath until 6 January. There was no love lost between the Campbells and the MacDonalds, and Dalrymple decided to use Maclan's tardiness an excuse to demonstrate the power of the crown. Accordingly, he sent a regiment of soldiers, commanded by another Campbell – Captain Robert Campbell of Glenlyon – to Glencoe. Apparently, Maclan interpreted the visit as a sign that he was now under the protection of the military, and extended a warm welcome to his assassins. The troops stayed with the MacDonalds for two weeks before falling on their hosts as they slept, butchering thirty-nine of them. Arguments may be concocted for viewing the massacre within the context of the time but, undeniably, it was a bad business, and an act which could only serve to heighten the already formidable distance between Highlanders and the seat of government.

Not only the Highlanders had reason to feel dissatisfied with William's policies. His preoccupation with waging war against France was to the liking of neither Highlanders nor Lowlanders, the ties between Scotland and France having survived for centuries. When William died, in 1702, to be succeeded by his sister-in-law, Anne – the younger daughter of James VII – English participation in the War of the Spanish Succession ensured that hostilities with France continued, and Scotland's trading links with Europe suffered accordingly. An attempt by the Scots to establish, at crippling cost, a trading base on the Isthmus of Darien in Central America, had been scuppered by William in order to preserve his alliance with Spain. As far as the economy was concerned, Scotland was on her knees.

Relations between England and Scotland reached breaking point when, without reference to Scotland, the English parliament proclaimed that when Anne – whose fifteen children all predeceased her – should die, she would be succeeded by Sophia of Hanover who, in turn, would have to subscribe to the tenets of the Church of England. So critical was the situation that there was no escaping the choice which had to be made: either Scotland should become entirely independent of England or the two countries should unite completely. A compromise, of sorts, was reached with the Scots agreeing to the creation of a single kingdom, and to the succession, upon Queen Anne's death, of the House of Hanover. The Presbyterian Kirk, together with the legal and education systems in Scotland would remain distinct and, significantly, Scotland was promised generous aid to revive her flagging economy. The Act of Union took effect on 1 May 1707, thus completing, at long last, the project begun by James I and VI a century before. However, within all unions, some member states are more equal than others, and there was no doubt that Scotland's interests would be subservient to those of her senior partner.

What had initially appeared to be a disaster for the Jacobite cause, therefore, might yet be turned to advantage, provided that anti-unionist factions could be drawn together. Although this was never likely to happen – for a return to a full-blooded Stuart monarchy meant a return to Roman Catholicism, which was anathema to most Scots – Louis XIV did sponsor a projected invasion of Scotland in 1708. Led, nominally, by James Edward Stuart, son of James VII, who had died in 1701, the expedition was prevented from making a landing by the English fleet. Similar plans for the following year failed to get further than the drawing board. The most opportune time to mount such an operation would always be immediately after the death of the reigning monarch, and when Queen Anne died in 1714, the 'Old Pretender', as James Edward came to be known, looked anxiously across the English Channel for a sign that his moment had come.

The Road to Sheriffmuir

Initially, the Old Pretender suffered a disappointment when the coronation of Britain's first Hanoverian monarch, George I, went off quietly. However, Jacobite hopes were raised when it transpired that George's main interests, like William's, centred on Europe and, in particular, in the development of the comparatively modest Kingdom of Hanover. Furthermore, he had little sympathy for the Tories, who were dismissed from and denied appointment to public office – all at a time when their interests, especially in Scotland, were suffering as a result of economic depression.

One of the most disgrunted of the out of favour Tories was John Erskine, Sixth Earl of Mar. Having done his best, as Secretary of State for Scotland, to ensure a smooth transition of power at the time of George's accession, he had some justification for being upset when his new master favoured him with a preview of his future status by turning his back on him at court. Instead of retiring gracefully to reminisce about the good times, Mar, a proud man, began a rebellion of his own.

Mar left London by collier and, disembarking at Newcastle, made his way to Fife, a hotbed of Tory discontent and a potential source of Jacobite support. From Fife, he rode north to drum up support among the Highland clans, succeeding to the extent that on 6 September 1715, at Kirkmichael – fittingly, only a few miles from Killiecrankie – he was able to raise the Jacobite standard.

Many reasons have been put forward for the failure of the '15 Rebellion, but the most decisive factor must be the death of Louis XIV, who had expired just a few days earlier. Momentarily occupied with their own

John Erskine, Earl of Mar, who
earned the nickname 'Bobbing John'
through his habit of changing sides.
(Mary Evans Picture Library)

problems, the French were in no position to provide James Edward with the
organization he needed to support Mar. Thus, although James and Mar
have both been criticized for not acting with enough speed, the run of play
was against them.

The government forces in Scotland were headed by John Campbell,
Second Earl of Argyll, an experienced commander, whose 3,000 or so
troops were outnumbered by more than two to one. By positioning himself
at Stirling, he hoped to stop Mar from linking up with other Jacobite forces
raised in the Lowlands and Northumberland – commanded by Viscount
Kenmure and Northumberland's MP, Thomas Forster. Instead of
challenging Argyll, Mar settled in at Perth and contented himself with
despatching between one and two thousand men under Brigadier William
Mackintosh to make contact with Kenmure and Forster. Mackintosh
achieved his objective at Kelso on 22 October 1715 and, again, the Jacobites
have been criticized for not marching on Stirling: Mar from the north and
Kenmure and Forster from the south. But Stirling Castle had proved its
impregnability on many an occasion, and a prolonged siege was out of the
question. Furthermore, the existence of a second government force under
Lieutenant-General George Carpenter, operating out of Newcastle, was
causing some concern, and so Forster, who seems to have taken command,

decided to march south into Lancashire where he hoped to rally considerable support. In terms of recruitment, his progress through Kendal, Penrith and Lancaster was disappointing, yet the army arrived, unscathed, at Preston on 10 November, where it rested.

On this same day, Mar finally decided to forsake the comforts of Perth and march south. Recruitment had been brisk – he now had some 10,000 men at his command – so he could afford to despatch 3,000 under General Alexander Gordon with orders to occupy the Earl of Argyll by making diversionary crossings of the Forth in the neighbourhood of Stirling, while the main Jacobite force crossed the river further upstream. Hearing of the plan, Argyll promptly marched out of Stirling to block Gordon's path 5 miles to the north, at Dunblane.

The Battle of Sheriffmuir

Argyll spent the evening of 12 November 1715 on Sheriff Muir, about 2 miles to the east of Dunblane. With Argyll on the move, Mar was forced to modify his plans and, having been rejoined by Gordon, he set out for Dunblane, encountering the Hanoverians on the frosty Sunday morning of 13 November.

Argyll's total strength remained at around 3,000 men. His infantry was deployed in two lines – six battalions in the first, protected on both flanks by four squadrons of dragoons, and two battalions in the second, each flank protected by a single squadron of dragoons. Command of the infantry was given to General Wightman, with General Witham commanding the dragoons on the left – Argyll himself retaining command of the right wing.

The Hanoverians, faces to the east, were ranged across high ground, but the undulating terrain before them meant that Argyll remained partially unaware of Mar's deployment – which was, in fact, very similar to his own, although on a larger scale. The Jacobites, said to be 10,000 strong, formed up in two lines of ten battalions each. The left flank of the front line was protected by two squadrons of horse under General Hamilton, the right by three squadrons under Mar. Left and right flanks of the rear line were protected by the Angus Horse and Earl Marischal's Horse respectively. A third reserve line, in the rear, consisted of 800 men, in itself one quarter of Argyll's total strength.

Accounts of the battle are conflicting and reflect, in some measure, the confusion which arose from Mar's hasty advance. His front-line infantry, commanded by Gordon, was made up of Highlanders. As usual, they were straining at the leash and, when the Hanoverians came into view, they launched a furious assault. However, that same undulating landscape which had blocked Argyll's view of Mar's deployment may also have led to uncertainty on Mar's part as to Argyll's true position, for the Jacobite army was to be seen advancing 'off-centre', in that its right wing generously overlapped the Hanoverian left. Argyll, too, noticed that unmanned territory opened up before his own right wing. Both commanders appear to have been over-anxious to exploit the opportunity for outflanking one another. Argyll charged forward with his dragoons and detachments of Wightman's infantry but, although Hamilton's wing was pressed back, its retreat was orderly and the Hanoverians were made to fight for every inch of ground. Mar's complementary attack on the Hanoverian left wing went much more smoothly, with his dragoons and Highlanders creating a whirlwind which swept Witham from the field.

While Witham was in full flight to Stirling, the Jacobite left had been pushed back behind its own lines as far as Kinbuck. It came as a surprise to each commander to learn that he was not the victor and, by all accounts, both hurried back to the battlefield to find it deserted. Argyll dug in and awaited Mar's attack for, although the numbers on both sides were much reduced, Mar retained some numerical superiority, although perhaps not to such an extent as one is sometimes led to believe. After all, it was in Argyll's interests to over-estimate the size of the Jacobite force facing him, just as it was in Mar's interests to exaggerate the numbers of men flocking to his banner. However, as the light began to fail, the ever cautious Mar withdrew to the parish of Ardoch, about 5 miles to the north-east of Dunblane, giving Argyll a chance to retreat to Dunblane itself.

Losses may have been about even, with 300–400 dead on each side, but as Argyll occupied the battlefield the following Monday morning, the victory should be ascribed to the Hanoverians. As far as the Jacobites were concerned, a contest drawn was as good as a battle lost, for Mar needed nothing less than a decisive victory to maintain the impetus of his revolt.

The battle had been a curious affair and, unless Mar's force was much smaller than has been claimed, it is difficult to believe that the battlefield was left deserted by the action on the wings. Some of Mar's cavalry stood aloof from the fighting and, with many of the front-line Highlanders breaking ranks to follow up Mar's assault on Witham, Wightman's infantry would have been better able to stand its ground. It is more likely that the commanders returned to the field to find what was essentially a stand-off situation which neither felt able to exploit.

The Aftermath

On the same day that Mar failed to make the most of his opportunity at Sheriffmuir, Forster was squandering his at Preston. Two days after his arrival, he learned that government troops under Generals Carpenter and Wills were approaching. Wills was first on the scene, to discover the approaches to the town, including the bridge over the River Ribble, unguarded. However, barricades spanned the narrow streets at each of the main entrances and when Wills attacked on 12 November, his men came under heavy fire. At the end of the day, despite some fierce house-to-house fighting, all the barricades remained *in situ*.

On 13 November, General Carpenter arrived. Immediately, he took possession of the bridge and effectively reduced Preston to a state of siege. Forster, who had displayed little interest in the fighting, had no stomach for a prolonged confrontation and sued for peace. Around 1,500 Jacobites were taken prisoner. Less than two dozen, had been killed, but many had taken flight prior to Carpenter's arrival.

While the rebellion in his cause was thus rapidly drawing to a premature and rather unspectacular close, the Old Pretender[1] was frantically trying to organize a passage to Scotland. The Duke of Orléans, Regent of France during the minority of Louis XV, was unsympathetic and it is even said that the English Ambassador in Paris, the Earl of Stair, tried to have James assassinated. Yet, without the men and materials he needed, James managed to set sail from Dunkirk on 16 December 1715, docking at Peterhead on 22 December. Ill and dispirited, he made a furtive journey to Scone, where plans for his coronation were cut short by the news that Argyll, commanding a new army, was on the move.

This intelligence also forced Mar to evacuate Perth. With James and the remnants of his army, he marched north – but not before devastating much of the surrounding countryside. Aimed at hampering Argyll's advance on the city, it was a move which succeeded merely in creating anti-Jacobite feeling. Having withdrawn as far as the port of Montrose, James Edward, accompanied by Mar and others, sailed for the Continent.

The wretched survivors of the Jacobite army finally disbanded in March 1716, at Ruthven. Of the nobility implicated in the rising, only two were executed: Viscount Kenmure and the Earl of Derwentwater. Others forfeited their estates – thirty-eight in all – a procedure which, in addition to

---

1 James was still only twenty-seven years of age.

serving as a punishment, destroyed the economic base necessary to any future rebellion. Several leaders, including Forster and Brigadier Mackintosh, escaped – Forster by means of subterfuge and Mackintosh through use of force. As always, it was the rank and file which suffered. From the prisoners taken at Preston, about thirty English were executed, with most of the rest being transported to the American colonies. Scottish prisoners, held in Edinburgh Castle, were taken south for trial, to Carlisle – behaviour which made a nonsense of the Act of Union's provisions in respect of the Scottish legal system, and which led to the eventual release of all but one.

Among the participants in the '15, those who escaped the consequences of defeat were the Highlanders. In part, this was due to the impracticality of mounting a prolonged Highland winter campaign in the immediate aftermath. In the long term, the government contented itself with building more forts, together with the introduction of a programme for the construction of military roads in order to facilitate troop movements. For the moment, however, with the extension of an amnesty to all but the MacGregors – who had been persecuted for upwards of a century – the clans remained intact, a prime source of cannon fodder for the Stuart cause for many years to come.

The Walk

Distance: 7 miles (11.27 km)

Begin in Dunblane, at the cathedral (Pathfinder 370–782014) (Point A), where there is ample car parking space. The cathedral itself is famous for its stained glass which is all modern, most of the medieval stained glass of Scotland's churches having been destroyed at the Reformation. Of particular interest, in a panorama of stunning artistry, is the 1914–18 memorial window on the east wall of the chapter house depicting, in part, a First World War soldier with Bishop Maurice, who prayed with the army of Robert the Bruce before Bannockburn.

Leaving the cathedral, proceed down The Cross and bear left onto High Street (the B8064). Follow High Street out of the town to its junction with the A9. Cross over the roundabout into Glen Road and continue to the junction with Kippenross Home Farm (Pathfinder 370–793003). Turn left here, to walk up to the battlefield. The point on the ascent marked by Lynns Farm (Pathfinder 371–815012) indicates the probable position of the Hanoverian right wing. The 'Gathering Stone', from which vantage point

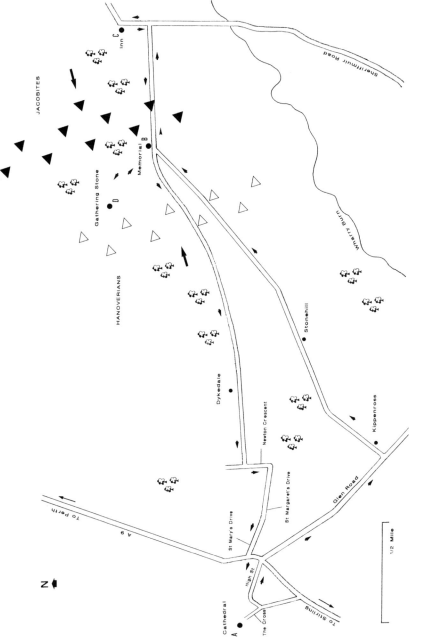

The Battle of Sheriffmuir, 1715

The MacRae memorial, Sheriffmuir.

Argyll surveyed the ground before him, and which marks the position of his left wing, is enshrouded in the trees to the north.

Further along the road is the battlefield monument (Pathfinder 371–815019) (Point B), a substantial stone structure, dedicated to the MacRae Clan and erected in 1915 by the Clan MacRae Society. According to the inscription, the MacRaes, forming part of the left wing of the Highland army, fell almost to a man. They must have occupied the ground in the vicinity of the monument and, from this point, one may look down on Lynns Farm to note their vulnerability to a Hanoverian outflanking manoeuvre.

Continue walking and, at the junction ahead, bear left to discover, set back in a clearing and sheltered to the west and north by the trees, the Sheriffmuir Inn (Pathfinder 371 – 827022) (Point C). Here one may take refreshment and admire the majestic peaks to the east. Before setting off back down the road, it is worth continuing a little further to see the four standing stones on rising ground to the right and – to the left – a portion of Sheriff Muir in its original treeless state.

After doing so, one may retrace one's steps to the monument, en route to the Gathering Stone. As late as 1973, in his *Guide to the Battlefields of Britain and Ireland*, Howard Green could comment, with some justification, on the difficulty of locating the Gathering Stone. Happily, today there is no such problem, for a path connecting it with the monument has been opened up. Follow this path, between the trees on one's left and the field boundary on the right, until it veers away to the left across the clearing to terminate at the Gathering Stone itself (Pathfinder 371–811022) (Point D). Protected by a rusty iron grille, it is situated on a spot which would have provided Argyll with as good a view as any of the landscape before him. Although the area is now quite thickly wooded, some thinning has taken place in recent years, and the ground immediately in front of the Gathering Stone is quite open.

Return to the monument once more, and instead of following the road back to Dunblane, take the track, beginning at the rear of the monument, through the woods. In fact, the route borders the trees and one is in sight of the road for much of the way. One emerges fully into the open as one approaches Dykedale Farm (Pathfinder 370–798004), on the site of which stood a building occupied by Argyll on the eve of the battle. Beyond the farm, one approaches the built-up area. Bear left into Newton Crescent, continuing via St Margaret's Drive and St Mary's Drive to the A9. To the left is the roundabout linking the A9 with the B8064 (High Street) which one may follow back to the cathedral.

Further Explorations

As a glance at Pathfinder 371 will show, the area to the north-east promises some splendid hill walking. In particular, the road between the Sherriffmuir Inn and Blackford (Pathfinder 371–897070) provides the rambler with a flavour of hill walking with no deviation from a metalled surface. Blackford was one of the villages burned by Mar in the aftermath of Sheriffmuir.

To the west, running parallel with this road, is a section of the A9 – the whole route connecting Stirling with Perth. This specific portion, Roman-like in its straightness, is identified as an 'Old Military Road' (Pathfinder 371–815055). However, it is not one of General Wade's projects, for Wade was succeeded as roadmaker by General Clayton who built this road, running from Stirling to Crieff, between 1741 and 1742. It must be said that much of the credit for the quality of the military roads in Scotland must go to William Caulfeild, Inspector of Roads from 1732 to 1767. Responsible for building 800 miles of military roads at a cost of £167,000 during his lengthy career, Caulfeild demonstrated considerable engineering skills in the building of bridges, some forty of them for Wade alone. The

The Borestone, Sheriffmuir. Note the fresh
floral tribute of the White Cockayde Society.

clan chieftains knew that the new roads would, in time, weaken the power
they wielded over their vassals, whose complaints centred on the gravel
surfaces which were hard on the unshod feet of their horses – and, indeed,
upon their own naked feet. Although he was given none of the credit for his
work, Caulfeild was granted the deputy-governorship of Inverness Castle
and maintained a friendly relationship with Wade, after whom he named
his eldest son.

Along the Stirling–Crieff road, to the north of Dunblane, is Balhaldie
House (Pathfinder 371–812051). Prince Charles Edward stayed there in
1745. Six months later, when Cumberland was pursuing the defeated
Jacobites after Culloden, a serving girl from Balhaldie House threw a pan of
boiling oil at the duke, narrowly missing him.

The only other road of any consequence leading north from Dunblane is
the B8033, leading circuitously to Braco, where it joins the Old Military
Road. Three miles from Dunblane, along the B8033, is Kinbuck. After
Sheriffmuir, the bridge across Allan Water, to the north of the village
(Pathfinder 370–792054) was held by Rob Roy and his MacGregors to
cover the retreat of Mar's army – an act which, although sensible, earned
them censure for having arrived late and failing to join the fighting.

To the west of Dunblane is the large village of Doune (Pathfinder

370–727016), once famed for its manufacture of Highland pistols. Doune Castle (Pathfinder 370–728011) is generally reckoned to be one of Scotland's best preserved medieval castles. Situated on relatively low ground, overlooking the River Teith, it was built during the late fourteenth century for Robert Stewart, 1st Duke of Albany and Regent of Scotland in the reign of Robert III. In 1425, the 2nd Duke, Murdoch Stewart, was executed and ownership of the castle passed to the crown, in the person of James I. In 1570, during the civil wars, it was besieged and captured by the Earl of Lennox and subsequently returned to the Stewarts, who became the Earls of Moray. In 1645, the castle was occupied by Montrose who recognized the importance of its situation at the confluence of two important routes: the Edinburgh to Inverlochy and the Glasgow to Perth roads. In 1745, it was seized by the Jacobites and used by them as a prison. One of the prisoners, the Reverend John Home, captured at the Battle of Falkirk, escaped by the expedient – probably quite novel at the time – of lowering himself from a window by a rope of sheets. The relative ease with which Doune seems to have been taken would have disappointed its builders for, apart from the provision of formidable outer defences, its design included the failsafe device of a gatehouse which could be isolated and held from enemies both within and without the castle.

Further Information

The battlefield of Sheriffmuir is well off the beaten track – on the minor road which runs between the A9, near Blackford, and Glen Road, Dunblane. Car parking is available in The Haining, immediately to the rear of Dunblane Cathedral, while a little makeshift off-road parking may be found by the Mackay memorial on the battlefield itself.

Dunblane is easily accessible by rail, with regular trains from Aberdeen, Glasgow and Edinburgh – and a connecting service to London (Euston and Kings Cross). For details of National Express and Scottish Citylink coaches, telephone 0990–808080 and 0990–505050 respectively.

Two Ordnance Survey Pathfinder maps are required: No. 370 and No. 371. The Landranger map is No. 57.

Information about the area can be found in the *Loch Lomond, Stirling and the Trossachs Visitor's Guide*, obtainable from the Tourist Information Centre, Dumbarton Road, Stirling (telephone 01786–475019). An informative leaflet entitled *In and Around Dunblane & Sheriffmuir* is also available. Indeed, a visit to the Stirling Tourist Information Centre can be of assistance in one's explorations of a much wider area. Another useful publication to buy is the locally produced *Stirling and The Trossachs: An Illustrated Architectural Guide* by Charles McKean.

As the '15 Jacobite Rebellion culminated in the Battle of Sheriffmuir, one would think – quite mistakenly – that a wide range of further reading is available. Howard Green gives an account in his *Guide to the Battlefields of Britain & Ireland*, as does William Seymour in *Battles in Britain 1642–1746*. More comprehensive coverage is to be found in Christopher Sinclair-Stevenson's *Inglorious Rebellion: the Jacobite Rising of 1708, 1715 & 1719*, and in John Baynes's *The Jacobite Rising of 1715*.

9
THE BATTLE OF PRESTONPANS
21 September 1745

Introduction

It was often remarked among the contemporaries of James Edward Stuart that the Old Pretender had little enthusiasm for his own cause which, in the wake of the '15, appeared, once more, to be dead and buried. To some extent a victim of circumstance – especially of the strengthening of ties between Britain and France – he can hardly be blamed for the taciturn and gloomy disposition which accompanied him throughout his wanderings. No longer welcome in France, he sought refuge in Italy, awaiting a call from his agents in Scotland.

In the event, he did not have to wait for long, although the possibility of assistance arose from an unusual source: Charles XII of Sweden. As a result of steadily deteriorating Anglo-Swedish relations, it appeared that the Swedes were open to any offer which would enable them to strike a blow against George I. Subsequent assessments of the negotiations which took place between leading Jacobites and Swedish officials have led historians to the conclusion that the Swedes were interested only in using the Jacobite cause as a means of raising funds for purposes of waging war on the continent. As Charles was killed at the siege of Frederikshavn in December 1718, the truth will never be known. The superstitious might argue that the Stuarts were cursed, the bad luck rubbing off on anyone foolish enough to associate with them, but the fact that all Jacobite risings had ended in unmitigated disaster did not deter others from continuing to risk life, limb and livelihood in their service.

The year 1718 appeared to be one of promise, for hostilities also broke out between England and Spain, allowing Philip V to jump on the Jacobite bandwaggon. The plan was for James Butler, Duke of Ormonde to lead 5,000 Spanish troops in an invasion of England, while the Earl Marischal, with a force of only 307 Spaniards, invaded Scotland. It was a venture fated to end in anticlimax for, on 7 March 1719, Ormonde's fleet was wrecked off Cape Finisterre and although the Earl Marischal effected a landing, he was unable to attract much support. At Glenshiel, on 10 June 1719, the 1,000 or so Highlanders who had been persuaded to participate in the invasion were put to flight by a Hanoverian force commanded by General Wightman, leaving the shamefaced Spanish contingent to surrender.

★

The survival of Jacobitism in Scotland remained a source of constant worry to the Hanoverian administration – and rightly so, as future events would show. Disarming Acts, intended to deprive the Highlanders of their weapons proved impossible to enforce, General Wade pointing out that 'great Quantities of broken and useless Arms were brought from Holland and delivered up to the Persons appointed to receive the same . . .' . Furthermore, the famous network of military roads constructed by Wade – over 250 miles – between 1726 and 1737, might be used just as effectively by a Jacobite army as by government troops.

Throughout this period, Jacobitism remained dormant, awaiting a catalyst to endow the comatose spirit with fresh life. Activists waited in the wings, ready to capitalize on steadily deteriorating relations between England and France, but it was clear that what the movement needed most was a new figurehead. The Old Pretender lacked the personal charisma necessary to the success of any future rebellion, but he had two sons, the elder of whom, Charles Edward Stuart, possessed in full measure the personal attributes required to charm his way into even the most dour of Highland hearts. And so, the Old Pretender faded into the obscurity from which he had never fully emerged, to be replaced by the Young Pretender, a romantic hero beside whom – in the popular imagination at least – the likes of Wallace and Montrose would pale into insignificance.

The Road to Prestonpans

By 1643, the 'entente cordiale' between England and France had soured to the extent that Louis XV was ready to listen to new entreaties to help restore the Stuart dynasty. With apparent ease, an invasion army of 13,000 men was assembled at Dunkirk. The bulk of this force would launch a direct assault of London via the Thames, while 3,000 men, under the Earl Marischal, would make a diversionary attack on Inverness. The invasion fleet – having been joined by Prince Charles, arriving hotfoot from Rome – embarked in February 1644. Through harrassment by the English navy, under Admiral Sir John Norris, the advance faltered and then collapsed with the onset of a violent storm which wrecked many of the troopships.

Not to be thwarted, the 23-year-old prince made plans for a landing in Scotland during the following summer. At least he had influential contacts in Scotland – in particular, the Jacobite Association, a league of gentlemen committed to promoting the Stuart cause. Not all of the members were in favour of such a rash course of action as Charles proposed, estimating that perhaps as few as 4,000 would rally to his support. No further help in terms of men or money could be expected from the French, who did nothing more than tolerate his presence, and there really seemed to be no realistic prospect of success. If the grand undertaking of February had failed, how could a small, independent venture succeed?

However, if nothing else, Charles Edward was determined to set foot on Scottish soil, and with a commendable sense of purpose, he set about raising the necessary funds. By borrowing 180,000 livres and pawning his mother's jewels, he was able to equip a modest expedition. In addition, sympathizers put a frigate and escort ship at his disposal so that on 5 July 1745, accompanied by a handful of followers, he was able to set sail – hopefully for the Isle of Mull. The venture nearly came to grief when a British warship engaged the escort off Lizard Point, disabling her to the extent that she was unable to continue. The prince's frigate carried on, arriving not on Mull but at Eriksay in the Outer Hebrides on 23 July 1745.

The welcome from the Highlanders was not as warm as Charles would have wished, several chiefs openly turning him down – in part because he had arrived alone but also because they had grown much warier in general about putting their trust in princes, especially those of the Stuart variety. Therefore, when he raised his banner at Glenfinnan on the mainland, it was in the presence of only 1,000 men. Without the backing of Donald Lochiel, who brought in 700 Camerons, the turnout would have been limited to 300 or so MacGregors.

The Hanoverian army in Scotland, commanded by Lieutenant-General Sir John Cope, itself comprised around 3,000 men, and the force Cope was actually able to field amounted to less than half that number. Yet, appreciative that the rising should be nipped in the bud, he marched westward, arriving at Corrieyairack Pass to the south of Fort Augustus on 27 August, to find that it was held by the Jacobites. Cope himself had been depending on the support of supposedly loyal Highland clans, but, like Charles, he, too, was disappointed. Unaware of the Jacobites' strength, he retreated to Aberdeen, leaving Charles a free road to the Lowland towns and cities.

While Cope evacuated his troops by sea, Charles pushed on via the Pass of Killiecrankie, to reach Perth on 4 September, where he recruited, among others, Lord George Murray. On 16 September, he by-passed Stirling, encouraged, no doubt, by fire from the castle's artillery. It might have been supposed that a similar attitude of defiance would have prevailed in

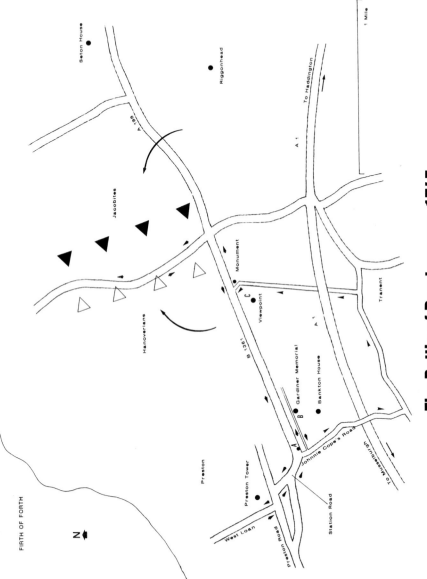

FIRTH OF FORTH

N

Seton House

Riggonhead

A 198

Jacobites

Hanoverians

Monument

Viewpoint

C

B 1361

Preston

Preston Tower

Gardiner Memorial

Bankton House

A

B

West Loan

Preston Road

Johnnie Cope's Road

Station Road

To Musselburgh

A 1

Tranent

A 1

To Haddington

1 Mile

The Battle of Prestonpans, 1745

Edinburgh, but this was not to be the case. Charles's demand for its surrender threw the town council into a panic and, while it dithered, the town was taken – the Jacobites entering with ease through an open gate on 17 September.

Meanwhile, Cope had sailed from Aberdeen to Dunbar, where he disembarked his army at the same time as the Jacobites were occupying Edinburgh. As soon as he learned of the landing, Charles commandeered as much in the way of arms and ammunition as he could lay his hands on, marching out to Duddingston, where, at a council of war, it was decided not to await Cope's inevitable approach but to advance to meet him.

The Battle of Prestonpans

On 19 September, Cope had marched from Dunbar to Haddington, where he spent the night. The following day, he set out on the next stage of his journey, initially following the course of the present-day A1 before making a detour to take him along the present-day A198 which ran through rather more open ground. The Jacobites, meanwhile, were on the road to Tranent and, on hearing of the proximity of Cope's army, Lord George Murray forged ahead to occupy Falside Hill, to the south-west of the town. He arrived to find the Hanoverian army on level ground to the north of Tranent, where Cope had decided to deploy his men when he, in turn, learned of the Jacobites' approach.

Cope was pleased with his position. Before him lay marshland, to his rear was the sea, while the park walls of the Preston and Bankton estates formed a barrier to the west. While the Jacobite leaders fell to discussions – often heated – among themselves as to how best to tackle the problem, Cope remained immobile. Unaware of the strength of the army opposing him, he dared not risk taking the initiative. At length, the Jacobites decided to outflank the marshland and, under cover of darkness, marched via Riggonhead, across the Longniddry road, to take up a position to the north-west of Seaton House. While crossing the marsh, Charles fell into the mud – a bad omen for a superstitious man.[1]

---

1   William the Conqueror had stumbled in the sand on landing at Pevensey Bay in 1066, prior to the Battle of Hastings. Unlike Charles Edward, William had the guile to turn the accident to his advantage by remarking that English soil was already in his grasp.

Towards daybreak, Cope realized what was happening and wheeled his army about to face due east. Although, in a sense, it might be argued that he had allowed himself to be boxed in, his position was still a strong one, with a ditch bordering the marsh to his right and the estate walls to his rear. Having been reinforced since landing at Dunbar, his army numbered about 2,500 men. His infantry comprised companies from the regiments of Murray, Lascelles, Guise and Lee. Two squadrons of Hamilton's dragoons protected the left flank, with two squadrons of Gardiner's dragoons on the right. On the extreme right wing was the artillery, while one squadron from each of Hamilton's and Gardiner's were held in reserve.

By this time, Cope must have realized that the strength of the opposition, standing at 2,400 men, was much lighter than he had anticipated. There had been much rivalry between the Jacobite Highlanders as to who should occupy pride of place on the right wing. In the end, the position was allocated to the MacDonalds so that, from right to left, the Jacobite line consisted of MacDonalds, the Duke of Perth's contingent, the MacGregors, the Stewarts of Appin and the Camerons. The Duke of Perth assumed command of the right wing, and Lord George Murray, the left. To the rear was a reserve, prominent among which were Murray's own Athollmen and the prince himself. Also in the rear were fifty cavalry under Lord Strathallen.

At dawn, the Jacobite army attacked, Murray's left wing leading the charge. There was a burst of fire from Cope's artillery before the gun crews, stricken with terror at the sight of the Camerons bearing down on them, abandoned their posts, Gardiner's dragoons quickly following suit. Colonel James Gardiner himself stood his ground until he was cut down by a Cameron axe. On the Jacobite right, the MacDonalds created similar panic in the Hanoverian ranks. To the surprise of observers, their advance, while menacing, was at once both uniform and orderly, and it was this precision as much as anything which succeeded in overawing the enemy. When Hamilton's dragoons turned tail, the infantry, with no protection, was left to bear the brunt of the onslaught. Many of the Camerons had quitted the field, in pursuit of Gardiner's dragoons, but some – again demonstrating remarkable discipline – turned in on the infantry. Cope, riding up and down the line, did his best to rally his men, but as soon as the broadsword-wielding Highlanders made contact with his infantry, there could be only one outcome.

Cope's strong defensive position had turned into a death trap, with his men, infantry and dragoons alike, being slaughtered as they fell back to the parkland walls in their rear. He did manage to organize some 450 survivors whom he led in an orderly retreat to Berwick, to be met there by a rival colleague who allegedly remarked that Cope must have been the first general in history to arrive before the news of his own defeat.

A contemporary print depicting Lord Mark Kerr's reception of General Cope, following the Battle of Prestonpans. Although news of Cope's defeat preceded his arrival at Berwick, the observation traditionally accredited to Kerr (see p. 113) captures the spirit of the occasion. (British Museum)

The Aftermath

Within a timespan of fifteen minutes or so, Cope's army had been all but destroyed. Over 200 of his men were dead and 1,500 taken prisoner, which suggests that the pursuit was not especially bloodthirsty, although hundreds more were wounded, with most of the casualties occurring during the flight. With eye-witness accounts of battles growing more common, one becomes much more aware of the realities of war and of the horrific scene presented by an eighteenth-century battlefield, with severed heads, arms and legs and hideously mutilated torsos scattered over a wide area. The Jacobites lost between twenty and thirty dead and probably not more than about fifty wounded, casualties which would have resulted from the combined long-range artillery and musket fire in the moments before the Highlanders came to grips with their adversaries. The Duke of Perth and Lord George Murray ensured that the wounded of both sides received attention, messengers being sent to Edinburgh to procure surgeons. Apparently, the prince, in the best of spirits, refreshed himself on the battlefield, 'with the utmost Composure . . . amidst the deep and piercing Groans of the wounded and dying, who had fallen a Sacrifice to his ambition'.

Cope was later exonerated at an 'examination', which cannot have been far short of a court martial, when he blamed his failure simply on the panic experienced by his men. He might have mentioned poor training and a consequent lack of discipline as contributory factors.

On 22 September, the Jacobite army, with Charles at its head, made a triumphant entry into Edinburgh, the prince taking up residence in Holyrood Palace, while his men later settled into camp at Duddingston. For six weeks, Charles was involved in a hectic round of social engagements, while Murray and Perth – without his interference – tried to consolidate the Prestonpans victory. Cope's baggage train had proved a valuable asset, containing cash, arms and supplies, but much booty had been carried off by clansmen who, true to form, slipped away soon after the battle, leaving Charles with a force only 1,500 strong. Arguably, much of Scotland was now under Jacobite control, yet the Highland forts and several castles, including Stirling and Edinburgh, remained firmly in government hands. While Charles held court at Holyrood, the garrison of Edinburgh Castle continued to receive supplies from the townsfolk, and while the prince's messengers roamed the Highlands, canvassing for support, the Hanoverian troops remained shut up in their barracks: all in all, a curious state of affairs.

As far as Scotland was concerned, recruitment was slow but steady, Prestonpans having transformed a no-hope venture to one with definite possibilities. The MacKinnons from Skye, the Macphersons of Cluny and Lords Lewis Gordon, Ogilvy, Pitsligo, Elcho and Kilmarnock, among others, all helped to swell the Jacobite numbers to 5,500, of which 500 were cavalry. The French, also cheered by the recent successes, sent more arms and supplies, accompanied by, as observer, the Marquis d'Eguilles. As encouraging as these events might be, the crucial factor was the situation in England. Would the English Jacobites recognize this as the main chance and come out in sympathy? Charles felt they would and wanted to march to Newcastle to challenge General Wade. Murray thought otherwise and persuaded the Prince to advance into England by the west coast route, the '15 having shown that the men of Lancashire were open to persuasion.

As far as Charles, or any Stuart pretender for that matter, was concerned, the occupation of Scotland remained strictly a means to an end. The primary objective would always be England, and on 3 November 1745, the Jacobite army set out from Dalkeith for the border.

The Walk

Distance: 5 miles (8.05 km)

Begin at Prestonpans railway station (Pathfinder 407–393738) (Point A), a suitable starting point for motorists and rail travellers alike. Cross the railway line by either the footbridge over the track or the underpass (Johnnie

Cope's Road) to the right. Once across, bear left to walk along the path skirting the south side of the railway line. Obscured by the trees, to the rear of Bankton House, is the Gardiner Monument (Pathfinder 407–395738) (Point B). Bankton was Colonel James Gardiner's home, and it seems strange that he should have met his end less than a mile away. It is said that he foretold his demise on the battlefield, although it is worth noting that having been seriously ill for some time, he may have had good reason for being preoccupied with thoughts of death.

Return to Johnnie Cope's Road and turn to the left, following the route by which General Cope made good his escape. Bankton House (Pathfinder 407–395737), once a ruin, has been painstakingly restored by the Lothian Building Preservation Trust and, at the time of writing (1996) is up for sale. After crossing the A1 via the bridge, continue to the junction and turn to the left again, to walk in the direction of Tranent. At the next junction lies the parish church of Tranent, within the confines of which lies Colonel Gardiner's unmarked grave. Take the path to the left, following the track of a waggonway, constructed in 1722 to service Tranent's opencast mine workings. The waggons, laden with coal, extracted from the site by women and children working under the most atrocious conditions, would freewheel down to the harbour at Cockenzie. It is recorded that in 1547, during the Battle of Pinkie, these same tunnels provided a place of refuge for the local populace.

The Gardiner Monument, to the rear of Bankton House, Prestonpans.

Continue under the A1 via the underpass, to be confronted, on emerging at the other side, by a grassy mound (Pathfinder 408–402739) (Point C) rising unnaturally from the level landscape. It seems unfair to describe it for what it is – a landscaped slag-heap – for it forms part of an attractive recreational area created literally, one might say, from the ashes of the opencast workings. The steep climb to the top is well worth the effort expended for there, on the crest, is a platform with plans of the Prestonpans campaign, and of each stage of the battle. To the east is Riggonhead, indicating the route by which the Jacobites outflanked Cope's original position. To the north is the battlefield itself, where the armies faced one another on either side of the present-day B6371.

Descend the mound and continue to the A198, to view the battlefield monument (Pathfinder 408–403742) standing by the bridge. Although the area has retained an open aspect, twentieth-century housing development on the opposite side of the A198 led to the unearthing of the remains of some of the battle's casualties, and these were reinterred where the monument now stands.

Continue along the A198 towards Preston,[2] following the line of the Hanoverian deployment on the night of 20 September 1745. Walk past the railway station, bearing right into Station Road to view the remains of Preston House (Pathfinder 407–391739), to where many of the wounded were taken after the battle. Preston House belonged to the Hamilton family, as did Preston Tower (Pathfinder 407–390740), a fifteenth-century tower house which was burned by Cromwell during the Dunbar campaign of 1650. Restored and owned by the National Trust for Scotland, its remains, a local landmark, may be visited by walking a little further up Station Road – after which one may retrace one's steps to the railway station and starting point.

Further Explorations

To the north of the battlefield of Prestonpans is the Firth of Forth and the beaches of Seton Sands and Gosford Sands. Words such as 'stunning' and 'captivating' are often used to describe East Lothian's beaches. To anyone

---

2 Although the final battle positions may be viewed from the vantage point, one may wish to extend the walk by making a detour – as suggested by the sketch-map – along the present-day B6371, to traverse the ground occupied by the combatants.

acquainted with the sandy coves of Devon and Cornwall, however, the Lothian coast has a bleak, almost forbidding air. Twentieth-century evidence of its vulnerability to coastal attack survives in the concrete pillboxes still to be found punctuating the landscape at intervals – for example, in the picnic area at Seton Sands (Pathfinder 408–431762). Seton does boast the remains of a fine collegiate church (Pathfinder 408–418751) founded in 1450 and which – as a glance at the map will show – can be visited by making a short detour during the suggested battlefield walk.

A little further eastwards are the remains of Redhouse Castle (Pathfinder 408–4637700), a tower house of particular interest through its surviving 'barmkin' or outer defensive wall and associated outbuildings. Similar structures may be viewed at Garleton Castle (Pathfinder 408–509768) and Barnes Castle (Pathfinder 408–529766), known as 'The Vaults' because it remained uncompleted, work not having progressed much beyond a series of vaulted basements.

No historical exploration of East Lothian would be complete without a visit to Haddington (Pathfinder 408–512739). Arguably East Lothian's oldest town, founded in the twelfth century, Haddington suffered greatly in all the major Anglo-Scottish wars, especially during the period of the 'rough wooing'. In 1548, in the aftermath of the Battle of Pinkie, the Duke of Somerset decided to turn Haddington into an English stronghold, from which the surrounding countryside could be controlled. Lord Grey of Wilton, to whom the task fell, oversaw the construction of an earth and timber wall, designed to surround the town and its garrison of 2,500 men. Towards the end of June 1548, a strong Franco-Scottish army surrounded Haddington, but stout resistance enabled the defenders to hold out until reinforced by the Earl of Shrewsbury. Despite the temporary relief occasioned by Shrewsbury's arrival, the winter of 1548–9 saw the English penned up in Haddington as a result of continuous enemy harassment. Somerset realized that his plan had failed. Haddington's inland location meant that it could not easily be supplied and, with many of the defenders suffering from the effects of disease and malnutrition, it was decided to evacuate the garrison and abandon the defences – nothing of which survives.

Over to the south-west of Prestonpans is Dalkeith (Landranger 66–3367), a small town which visitors to the Lothians usually miss. Dalkeith Palace (Landranger 66–334679), built in the early eighteenth century, home of the Dukes of Buccleuch, accommodated Prince Charles Edward for two nights, prior to his celebrated march into England. Of the earlier Dalkeith Castle, belonging to the Douglas family, and which occupied the same site, there is no trace. General Monck governed Scotland from Dalkeith Castle for Cromwell during the years of the Protectorship, and it was from here that Monck made his plans for the Restoration.

Four miles further south-west is the village of Roslin and the ruins of Roslin Castle (Landranger 66–275628), built in the fourteenth century by Sir William Sinclair. It was at Roslin, during Edward I's 1303–4 Scottish campaign, that John Comyn and Simon Fraser inflicted severe damage upon the English army. In 1544, the castle was burned by Hertford in the course of his punitive expedition to Edinburgh and Leith, suffering again at the hands of Monck a century later.

Further Information

The town of Prestonpans is situated on the B1361, between Edinburgh and North Berwick. It is best approached via the Wallyford turn-off on the A1 (Pathfinder 407–363712), from which it is a straight run along the A6094/B 1361 to Preston and the railway station. The best day for a visit is Sunday, when the station is quiet. Dominating the skyline is the Power Station by Cockenzie Harbour.

Rail users may travel from Edinburgh to Prestonpans, telephone 0131–556–2451 for details of services. The Sunday service is very limited, so that a weekday visit is advisable if this mode of transport is preferred. A half-hourly bus service, with a stop at Prestonpans, operates throughout the week, including Sundays. For further information, telephone 0131–654–0707.

Two Ordnance Survey Pathfinders are needed: Nos. 407 and 408 – the suggested walk being almost equally divided between them in terms of length. The relevant Landranger map is No. 66.

The general tourist literature makes little mention of Prestonpans, and more could be done to publicize the splendid battlefield viewpoint and accompanying pictorial display. However, the *East Lothian Holiday Guide*, available from the Tourist Information Centre at Old Craighall Service Area, near Musselburgh, is worth consulting, together with the *East Lothian: Visitor Attractions and Activities* booklet (telephone 031–653–6172). Preston Tower, a National Trust property, is open all year.

In its role as an important encounter of the '45, the Battle of Prestonpans warrants inclusion in all the major studies of the rebellion. A useful account is to be found in *Battles of the '45* by Katherine Tomasson and Francis Buist, and another in Jeremy Black's *Culloden and the '45*. In addition, Philip Warner's *British Battlefields: Scotland and the Border* contains a short, readable account.

10
THE BATTLE OF FALKIRK
17 January 1746

Introduction

The defeat of the Hanoverian army at Prestonpans occasioned as much panic at Westminster as the Highlanders had created among Cope's infantry. In the aftermath of the battle, while the Jacobites were engaged in building up their strength, the English government, with rather more ease, was also busily assembling its scattered forces. The Dutch, allies of England in the War of the Austrian Succession (1740–8), sent the first of 6,000 troops to England and the Duke of Cumberland's army was recalled from Flanders. Once assembled, this substantial army was divided into three groups: one, under General Wade, was despatched to Newcastle; the second, under Lieutenant-General Sir John Ligonier, marched into Lancashire; the third remained in the south-east to defend the English capital. Wade's group alone, consisting of over 10,000 men, dwarfed the Jacobite army, and the fact that so many government troops could be put in the field was sufficient to encourage virtually all Jacobite sympathizers to keep their own counsel.

Fortunately for Prince Charles, Wade, 73 years old and ailing, was not up to the job. Ill-health had compelled him to return from Flanders in 1744 and it cannot have been envisaged that he would have to take up arms again. In fact, Wade expected a head-on clash with the Jacobites at Newcastle, but although Lord George Murray, accompanied by Charles, advanced into Northumberland, it transpired that this was merely a subterfuge, to cover the advance of the main column, under the Duke of Perth, which marched via Moffat and Lockerbie into Cumberland. At Jedburgh, Murray turned south-west, joining up with the Duke's column to the north of Carlisle.

Carlisle's defences had deteriorated substantially since the far-off days of the border wars and, moreover, was poorly defended by the local militia. Initially, in the expectation that Wade's cavalry would be riding to the rescue, the garrison rebuffed Jacobite demands to surrender. But Wade sent a message to say he would not be coming, and although a handful of professionals determined to hold the castle, the townsfolk, fearful of Jacobite claims that 16,000 men were ready to overrun the community, insisted on the surrender of both castle and city. In fact, Wade did try to get through but at Hexham his progress was halted by a combination of bad weather and bad roads. In short, the man responsible for building an efficient network of roads to facilitate troop movements in Scotland had been defeated, in part, by the poor condition of roads in England. Doubtless unappreciative of the irony of the situation, he returned to Newcastle.

Even without help, Carlisle should have been able to hold out for, as Wade had, in fact, suggested, Charles could not afford to embark on a prolonged siege. Such were the difficulties of holding together a Highland army that, since leaving Edinburgh, Charles had lost about 1,000 men who had no intention of fighting on 'foreign' soil. Nevertheless, with Carlisle subdued, the Jacobites were able to continue their march southwards in two divisions, the first commanded by Murray, the second by the prince.

On 22 November, they reached Manchester where they were received with much enthusiasm, but few offers of support. In the end, some 250 riffraff were recruited, forming the 'Manchester Regiment', commanded by Francis Towneley. The realists among the Jacobite leaders accepted that this was not enough. Only Charles, preoccupied with plans for his triumphal entry into London, remained buoyant. Murray was more concerned about Wade, who was finally marching southwards from Newcastle and Ligonier's column – now under the command of the Duke of Cumberland, Ligonier having fallen ill – moving into the Midlands.

Seemingly for no other reason than to humour the Prince, Murray and the Highlanders decided to march on to Derby. In order to avoid running into Cumberland, another diversionary march was deemed necessary, Murray leading a column in a south-westerly direction to Congleton, thereby giving Cumberland the impression that he was to be attacked. Under cover of Murray's feint, which stemmed Cumberland's advance, Charles proceeded to Derby where he met up with Murray again on 4 December. Beyond Derby, the clan chiefs would not venture, arguing that the absence of any anticipated support left them with no choice. Moreover, the Duke of Perth's brother, Lord John Drummond with 800 men had lately arrived at Montrose, lending credibility to the alternative way forward: that of consolidating the Jacobite position in Scotland. The prince could do little more than roundly abuse the counsel of those who had risked all in his cause adding, peevishly, that it was the last advice he would accept. As a contemporary had once remarked apropos James Edward, the Old Pretender, Charles's behaviour showed that he was 'of the family'.

The Road to Falkirk

It was a dispirited Jacobite army which, on 6 December 1745, began the long, homeward trek, with Murray assigning himself the most potentially vulnerable position in the rear. The consensus of opinion among historians is that the retreat effectively signalled the end of the '45 rebellion and that, had Charles covered the remaining 120 miles to London, he may have met with success. True, his risks to date had paid off, but Cumberland intended to block his path at Northampton. Even if this ruse failed there was yet another sizeable government force camped to the north of London, on Finchley Common, to be overcome. Clearly, the decision was strategically sound.

As many generals have discovered before and since, a retreating army is not quite so popular as an advancing army, and much of the warmth and enthusiasm which had greeted the Prince on the way south – particularly in Manchester – was now supplanted by disinterest or open hostility. The situation was not improved by Charles's insistence on making a leisurely withdrawal, for there remained the possibility that the rebels would be trapped between Wade and Cumberland. This did not happen because both Hanoverian forces had marched themselves to a standstill, Cumberland being further delayed by rumours of a French invasion. Had the rebels marched on London, perhaps the French would have pressed ahead with their plans, but it seems they were unable to solve the difficulties attendant upon transporting and disembarking horses.[1] In the end, the threat posed by the English fleet caused the attention of the French to be diverted from England to Scotland and, with the pressure on the south-east relieved, Cumberland was able to continue.

Inclement weather now hampered the progress of both pursued and pursuers, particularly that of the Jacobites whose artillery became bogged down in the mud. Travelling light, with a combined force of cavalry, dragoons and mounted infantry – 4,000 in all – Cumberland was able to make up ground, so that by 18 December, he was only a mile behind the Jacobite rearguard, comprising mainly the MacDonalds of Glengarry. With Charles and the vanguard already in Penrith, Murray had been forced to spend the night of 17 December in Shap, 10 miles away. On the following morning, as he pressed on to Penrith, advance parties of Cumberland's cavalry were sighted – the main force, he learned, being only a mile or so

1   A problem solved by William the Conqueror, seven centuries earlier.

Prince Charles Edward Stuart, 'Bonnie Prince
Charlie', as his supporters liked to see him. (National
Galleries of Scotland)

behind. At the hamlet of Clifton, only 3 miles short of Penrith, Murray
therefore decided to make a stand.

With his men deployed in and around the village, he received a message
from Charles to the effect that he must continue his withdrawal. Had he
obeyed this order, his party might well have been exterminated. Instead, he
waited for Cumberland to make the first move, which the duke did by sending
in 500 dragoons on foot under cover of darkness. The dragoons were detected
in the fitful moonlight but, as the Highlanders advanced stealthily to meet
them, an unexpected volley from the Hanoverian muskets stopped several
MacPhersons in their tracks. Recovering quickly, they charged the dragoon
line which, according to some accounts, stood its ground rather longer than
had been usual in such cases – a circumstance which, if accurate, must have
been of some concern to Murray. However, the dragoons did eventually retire
with losses of around forty killed and wounded. Murray admitted to having
lost just five men, although there were unsubstantiated reports of his having
thrown many casualties into the River Lowther in order to conceal the truth of
having suffered much heavier losses. Such was the skirmish of Clifton which,
apart from securing a safe passage into Scotland for Charles, has the
distinction of being the last battle fought on English soil.

Far from chastising Murray for disobeying orders, the prince expressed
pleasure at the outcome and resumed the march northward. A day was

spent at Carlisle where 400 men together with most of the column's artillery were, in effect, abandoned, supposedly to garrison the castle. Ten days later, on 30 December, Cumberland's heavy guns would force them to submit. Charles had wanted to retain a foot-hold in England for no reason other than to satisfy his foolish pride and, in so doing, had condemned many of his loyal followers to traitors' deaths.

The Jacobite army crossed into Scotland on 20 December and made straight for Glasgow, which it reached on Christmas Day. Charles's exorbitant demands for supplies and money did nothing to endear him to the hearts of the citizens, and on 3 January 1746, he left for Stirling. With the addition of Lord John Drummond's army and of another raised by Lord Lewis Gordon, the Jacobite army, according to the highest estimates, now comprised 9,000 men. Government figures put the number at 6,500 which may be more realistic after allowing for desertions among Highlanders who had followed Charles into England and who would have departed for their homes upon their return.

Over the preceding weeks, the government army had also been regrouping, and had succeeded in taking Edinburgh. Now, with Charles penned back in Scotland, the Duke of Cumberland, in response to the continuing French invasion scare, was sent back to the south of England, while Wade retired. The new man in charge of the offensive against the Jacobites was Lieutenant-General Henry Hawley, an unpopular disciplinarian highly thought of by Cumberland. As with the Jacobite army, it is likely that the strength of the forces under his command has been overestimated and that initially he, too, had about 6,500 fighting men at his disposal.

It had seemed probable that Charles would try to re-establish himself in Edinburgh, and so Hawley ensured that he arrived first, the advance guard of his army entering the town on 2 January 1746. Charles, however, was content to besiege Stirling Castle, and Hawley's desire for a speedy confrontation compelled him to make immediate arrangements to move on. His second-in-command, Major-General John Huske, left Edinburgh on 13 January, with Hawley and the artillery following two days later. By the evening of 16 January, the royal army was camped in fields to the west of Falkirk, Hawley and his staff officers enjoying the comforts of Callender House, the home of the Jacobite Earl of Kilmarnock.

The Battle of Falkirk

During the siege of Stirling Castle, Charles established himself at Bannockburn House, and in the final stages of Hawley's approach, it became customary for the Jacobite army to be paraded at Plean, 2 miles to the south-east of the prince's headquarters. At a council of war which took place on the morning of 17 January, Lord George Murray, as keen as ever to secure the advantage of high ground, suggested that the Hill of Falkirk, to the south-west of the town should be occupied. In a manoeuvre aimed at misleading Hawley, Drummond led one column down the main road to Falkirk, while Charles and Murray headed two additional columns on a detour across country. With Hawley's attention riveted – it was hoped – on Drummond, Charles and Murray would succeed in taking the hill. In fact, the stratagem was quickly discovered as the main Jacobite force was spotted crossing the River Carron, prior to its ascent of the hill. That the initial Hanoverian response was confused was due to the cunning of Lady Kilmarnock who ensured that Hawley was fully occupied in being lavishly wined and dined. When he finally appeared on the scene, Hawley ordered his men to beat the Jacobites to their objective.

Both sides reached the top at about the same time, deploying in the midst of torrential rain. With a ravine to the north and marshland bordering the Glen Burn to the south, outflanking actions by either side looked improbable and, but for the marsh, the royal dragoons might have played havoc among the Highlanders as they struggled to get into position.

The Jacobite army was deployed in two lines, the front line – from right to left – consisting of MacDonalds, Farquharsons, Mackenzies, Mackintoshes, MacPhersons, Frasers, Camerons and Stewarts. In the second line were battalions of the Atholl Brigade, with battalions of Lord Ogilvy's and Lord Lewis Gordon's. Drummond's diversionary force, arriving late, formed a reserve, flanked on either side by cavalry. Hawley also drew up his men in two lines: the infantry regiments of Wolfe, Cholmondeley, Pulteney, The Royals, Price and Ligonier in front; the infantry of Blakeney, Munro, Fleming, Barrel, Battereau and Howard to the rear. The most vulnerable regiments, the Argyll Militia and the Glasgow Volunteers – which had helped swell Hawley's numbers to 8,000 – were placed in relatively sheltered positions, the former in front of the ravine, the latter on the left wing, behind six squadrons of dragoons.

At about 4.00 p.m., before his regiments of foot had finished deploying, Hawley, who was determined to prove the superiority of cavalry over infantry, ordered his dragoons to attack. Lord George Murray, commanding on the Jacobite right, waited until the horsemen were almost upon him before giving the order for his men to fire, the resulting volley all but destroying the advance. Those dragoons who did break through had their horses cut out from under them and the MacDonalds went off in pursuit of many of the remainder who were in full retreat, having dispersed in their flight much of their own left wing, including the Glasgow Volunteers.

The fighting now became confused. After firing their muskets once, the Highlanders down the line cast their firearms aside and, as was their custom,

fell to with their swords. As on so many occasions in the past, the opposition crumbled, most of the government infantry in both front and rear lines taking to its heels. Only Ligonier's, Price's and Barrell's regiments on the right, afforded some protection from frontal attack by the ravine, stood their ground. The Jacobite left wing, lacking firm leadership, was thus unable to launch a charge and, in the face of desultory musket fire, had to retire. Undoubtedly, Ligonier's, Price's and Barrell's regiments saved the day, for they were even able to direct fire at the flanks of the Highlanders pursuing their fleeing comrades.

Much of the remainder of the fading afternoon light seems to have been spent in attempts by officers of both sides to rally their men. The Hanoverians were the first to leave, for although about a hundred dragoons had been rallied, the heavy rain rendered many muskets unserviceable. They expected the Jacobites to take up pursuit but, although Murray could still call on his reserves, most of his men were scattered far and wide. In the gathering darkness, he wisely decided to satisfy himself with taking possession of the field.

The Aftermath

On entering Falkirk, the Jacobites encountered almost no resistance. In his hurried retreat, Hawley had instructed his men to burn everything of value, yet the rain had rendered this impossible so that tents, clothing and other supplies fell into welcoming hands. However, only 1,500 Highlanders spent the night in Falkirk. The remainder were busy robbing the dead, or pillaging the abandoned Hanoverian camp, while more had returned to their quarters at Bannockburn, convinced that the battle had been lost.

Jacobite casualties in the action, which lasted not above half an hour, were assessed at fifty dead and up to eighty wounded while Hawley lost almost 600 officers and men killed, with many more wounded. At Linlithgow, where he sought refuge in the evening, Hawley's sentiments were much the same as those expressed by Cope after Prestonpans. Blaming his infantry for displaying 'suche scandalous Cowardice', he reported somewhat untruthfully to Cumberland: 'I can't say We are quite beat today.' Back in Edinburgh the following day, he exonerated himself from blame by having dozens of his men executed for cowardice and desertion. Several officers were court martialled, including the artillery commander, Captain Archibald Cunningham, whose guns – like those of the Jacobites – had become stuck in the mud and who had been unable to participate in the fighting.

The Jacobite high command also expressed concern at the poor discipline shown by the Highlanders, and there was more argument over the question of future plans. Charles insisted upon a return to the siege of Stirling Castle and while he repaired once more to Bannockburn House, Murray, with part of the army, remained in Falkirk. Here, the clan chieftains were in agreement that they should retreat into the Highlands to harry the forts and regroup to launch another expedition in the spring. Against this united front, Charles had no recourse but to throw another temper tantrum – in the course of which it is said that he banged his head against the wall until he reeled – and then did as he was told.

While plans were being made for the withdrawal, it was learned that the Duke of Cumberland had reached Linlithgow. Although Hawley had escaped official censure for his generalship at Falkirk, command of future operations was given to the Duke of Cumberland who had arrived in Edinburgh a fortnight after the battle. His preferment may well have owed rather more to his royal lineage than to any natural ability but, perhaps because of his royal blood, he enjoyed the confidence of his men. On 31 January, at the head of a new army, he left Edinburgh for Stirling and, he hoped, a showdown with the Jacobites. Charles would have obliged gladly, but for his having been overruled.

With Cumberland's rapid approach, the Jacobite retreat, which began on 1 February, was far less orderly than Murray would have preferred and included the loss of powder and other stores in an explosion. The evening of 1 February was spent in Dunblane and Doune, 3 miles to the west. The following night, at Crieff, there took place the most acrimonious council so far, at the end of which it was decided that the prince should accompany the Highlanders to Inverness via Pitlochry while Murray led the Lowland regiments towards the same objective along the coast road. Before setting out on 4 February, the Jacobites spiked and abandoned all their heavy guns. The weather was atrocious and food scarce – factors which affected both armies, causing Cumberland, 'for want of several necessaries', as he put it, to remain in Perth for two weeks. This time, nothing would be left to chance in the drive for complete annihilation of the Jacobite dream.

The Walk

Distance: 3 miles (4.83 km)

Begin in the grounds of Bantaskine Estate (Pathfinder 405–871789) (Point A), a public park with car parking facilities within. At the time of the '45, there was a Bantaskine House, but only the gardens have survived. From the car park on the right, follow the path a little further into the park to view the ravine (Pathfinder 405–871792) to the right. Eating far into the hillside, it formed an inpenetrable barrier for both the Jacobite left wing and the Hanoverian right wing.

Walk back, past the car park and out onto Lochgreen Road, turning to the right. Continue as far as Greenbank Road, on the corner of which is the battlefield monument (Pathfinder 405–868789) (Point B), bearing the inscription: 'The Battle of Falkirk was fought around here'. As with many such monuments, it seems to have been placed somewhat off-centre, for the fighting occurred rather more to the east. (One will also note the existence of a bridleway running away to the right, through the park, with a warning to indicate that it is intended for 'Permit Holders only' – an unusual limitation.)

Walk along Greenbank Road to the terminus of the Edinburgh and Glasgow Union Canal. To the left, at Tamfourhill, is the site of a Roman camp (Pathfinder 405–859794) and to the right, paths on either side of the canal – the towpath on the north bank and a footpath bordering the Bantaskine Estate on the south bank. Take the latter path and set off towards Falkirk.

The canal itself runs a distance of 30 miles between Edinburgh and Falkirk, with no locks. Opened in 1822 and abandoned by the British

The battlefield memorial, Falkirk.

Waterways Board in 1965, it is now associated with the leisure and tourist industry, as opposed to the heavy industries attendant upon opencast mining. A glance to the right as one proceeds will show that the ground is very uneven and broken up by several gullies. Continue to the foot-bridge (Pathfinder 405–878793) spanning the canal. Immediately to the north is Maggie Wood's Loan (Pathfinder 405–878796), the track by which the Hanoverian army hurriedly advanced from their camp around Arnott Hill (Pathfinder 405–882799), in the vicinity of the present-day infirmary.

Do not cross the bridge, but turn, instead, to follow the path to the rear of the Seagull Centre (a specialized facility to encourage use of the canal by the disabled) to open ground and a flight of steps etched into the side of the sharply rising ground. To the left of the steps are the remnants of walls which serve to remind one of past grandeur. Ascend the steps to walk into Sunnylaw Place and Myreton Way. Bear left at the end and then turn right into Lendrick Avenue. By bearing left at the top, one emerges onto Slamannan Road. Turn right to walk past the hospital, marking the centre of the Hanoverian lines which stretched away to the north, on land now occupied by the housing development one has just traversed, and to the south, beyond the development to the rear of the hospital.

Further along Slamannan Road (the B803), is another housing estate (Point C), cunningly built on what may well have been the site of the most crucial action of the battle: the Hanoverian dragoon charge on the Jacobite left wing. Continue along the road and ahead, beyond the line of trees stretching away to the right, is the ground occupied by the Jacobite army.

According to Pathfinder 405, it should be possible to traverse the centre ground by a track linking the B803 with Lochgreen Road, but only the suggestion of a stone wall, marking a vanished field perimeter (Pathfinder 405–860785) actually exists. A second track, 400 yards further on, (Pathfinder 405–867784) has also been consigned to obscurity for all time, so the only recourse is to retrace one's steps as far as Hillcrest Road, linking the B803 with Lochgreen Road which takes one back to Bantaskine Estate and the starting point.

Further Explorations

There is little visible evidence to suggest that Falkirk was once a walled town, with an eventful history, its rebirth as a child of the industrial revolution having led all too readily to the erasure of most traces of previous incarnations.

To reach back into the past, beyond reminders of the ironworkings and coal mining, one must confine one's attentions to the south of the town, and its Roman associations, embodied in surviving portions of the Antonine Wall. As indicated on the map (Pathfinder 405–932794), a short stretch fell victim to the M9 motorway but, near Beancross, the site of the largest fort along the wall, it remains virtually intact (Pathfinder 405–918795). To the north of Callendar Wood, over three-quarters of a mile has survived the ravages of development. Fortunately, two of the best sections are under the care of the National Trust for Scotland and Historic Scotland: at Watling Lodge (Pathfinder 405–865798) and at Rough Castle (Pathfinder 405–843798), the best preserved of the forts. An interesting feature of Rough Castle is the survival of a number of pits, in which sharpened stakes concealed with brushwood would be positioned as a further line of defence.

Falkirk was also prominent in the Wars of Independence, the first Battle of Falkirk (22 July 1298), fought between the armies of William Wallace and Edward I, taking place only a mile and a half away from what would be the site of the later Jacobite battle. Wallace's army, heavily outnumbered, formed up on the slopes of Callendar Wood, most probably to the east in the area now occupied by Woodend Farm (Pathfinder 405–902785). Edward, having spent three weeks searching for the Scots since crossing the border at the beginning of July, was keen to bring Wallace to battle. He divided his considerable force, comprising 2,500 heavy cavalry and up to 15,000 foot soldiers, into three 'battles': the vanguard under the joint command of the Earls of Norfolk and Hereford, the second under the Bishop of Durham and the third under Edward's own command. A stream, the Westquarter Burn, divided the two armies, and Wallace thought that the English knights would become bogged down in the marshland bordering the river. However, the Earls and the Bishop managed to gain firm ground by moving to left and right respectively. Although the Scottish pikes brought down many of the English horses, Edward brought up his archers, whose concentrated fire wrought gaps in the enemy lines which the cavalry was able to exploit, putting the Scots to flight. Wallace escaped into the forest, continuing on into exile and unwarranted disgrace.

Callendar House (Pathfinder 405–898794) has a history going back some 900 years. The estate came into the hands of the Livingstone family in the fourteenth century, where it remained until forfeited by James, 5th Earl of Linlithgow and 4th Earl of Callendar for demonstrating his Jacobite sympathies in the '15. However, it was later leased back to the family in the person of Lady Kilmarnock, who entertained General Hawley so purposefully prior to the second Battle of Falkirk (see p. 125). Quite recently in danger of falling into decay, Callendar House has now been restored and houses an exhibition based on its fascinating history.

Six and one half miles to the east of Falkirk is Linlithgow (Landranger 65–9977). Once one of the most important royal burghs in Scotland, the town's ancient thoroughfares have echoed to the march of many armies.

Edward I stayed here on the eve of his victory at the first Battle of Falkirk, and it was to Linlithgow that General Hawley retreated after his defeat at the second. Linlithgow Palace (Landranger 65–0077), begun in 1425 by James I, was birthplace to both James V and Mary, Queen of Scots. In the year after Culloden, when garrisoned by government troops, it was partially destroyed by fire. There remains some doubt as to whether the conflagration was accidental, for it may have been decreed that such a potent symbol of Scottish sovereignty should not be allowed to exist. It is with a sense of irony that one draws attention to one of the building's most imposing features: the magnificent fireplace, so wide that it is divided by pillars into three bays.

Further Information

To anyone unfamiliar with the locality, the site of the second battle of Falkirk is not easily accessible by road. Unusually, the battlefield is unmarked on the relevant Pathfinder (405), although the battlefield memorial is indicated (Pathfinder 405–868789). From Junction 4 of the M80, motorists should take the road to Bonnybridge, then follow the signs to High Bonnybridge. Continue through High Bonnybridge to Drum Wood (Pathfinder 405–832775), where the road bends sharply to take one, via Greenrig, to the Monument and on to the Bantaskine Estate – the narrow entrance to which appears unexpectedly on the left. The brave-hearted may wish to attempt a more direct route by tackling Falkirk's one-way system.

Falkirk is easily accessible by rail. Falkirk High Station is on the Edinburgh–Glasgow line, and from here, one may walk along Slamannan Road, into Lochgreen Road and on to the Bantaskine Estate. For details of National Express and Scottish Citylink Coaches, telephone 0990–808080 and 0990–505050 respectively.

An excellent publication is *The Forth Valley National Tourist Route*, available from the Tourist Information Centre, 2–4 Glebe Street, Falkirk (telephone 01324–620244). Although it still fails to mention the battle, it contains useful visitor information relating to local attractions, such as Callendar House and Linlithgow Palace. An additional range of well-produced leaflets is also available.

As already noted, the Ordnance Survey Pathfinder is No. 405. Landranger 64 also refers. The *Ordnance Survey Street Atlas of Glasgow & West Central Scotland*, which takes in Falkirk – and which does indicate the battlefield – is recommended. Further reading is provided by Katherine Tomasson and Francis Buist in *Battles of the '45* and by Jeremy Black's *Culloden and the '45*.

11
THE BATTLE OF CULLODEN
16 April 1746

Introduction

In retrospect, one may sympathize with the Young Pretender's frustration at his supporters' refusal to capitalize on their victory over the Hanoverian forces at the Battle of Falkirk. Since the decision to withdraw from Derby, the '45 rebellion had deteriorated into a continuous retreat until now, in mid-February 1746, the prince, despairingly, found himself trudging back to the far north of Scotland, to Inverness.

Both the Duke of Cumberland and Charles himself felt that the Jacobite challenge was over, yet several incidents demonstrated that the Highlanders were still a force to be reckoned with. For example, on 10 February, the garrison at Ruthven Barracks – comprising an officer and twelve men – surrendered to Charles's column, after which the stronghold was blown up. On the evening of 16 February, the prince, now only 8 miles short of Inverness, reached Moy Hall, where he was entertained by Lady Anne Mackintosh. His arrival came to the attention of John Campbell, Lord Loudon, commanding the government garrison of 2,000 men at Inverness. With one eye on glory and the other on the reward of £30,000 for Charles's capture, Loudon, accompanied by 1,500 men, stole out of the town to take the unsuspecting prince by surprise. Also residing in Inverness was the Dowager Lady Mackintosh whose strong Jacobite sympathies led to Loudon's undoing, for she managed to get a message through to Moy, ahead of the garrison commander's party. While Charles sought refuge some little distance from the Hall, Lady Anne persuaded a handful of men led by the village blacksmith to advance, yelling and firing muskets, on Loudon's approaching column. In the darkness, Loudon mistook them for a force superior to his own, and in what became known as the Rout of Moy, his men panicked and fled.

On the following day, when the prince's column appeared before

Inverness, Loudon decided to abandon the town, hurriedly retreating across the Moray Firth, with the Jacobite advance guard in hot pursuit. While Cumberland fumed, Charles established himself at Culloden House, about 5 miles to the east of the town, to await Murray's arrival. Lord George's exhausted column did not appear until 21 February, snowstorms having made progress very difficult, and forcing Murray to abandon yet more precious artillery.

With their backs to the wall, the only course open to the Jacobites was to attempt to consolidate their position. With this aim in view, Brigadier Walter Stapleton led a successful attack on Fort Augustus. For surrendering, the garrison commander, Major Wentworth, was later court martialled and dismissed from service. Before leaving, the Highlanders contrived to render the fort uninhabitable. A similar attempt on the strongly garrisoned Fort William proved unsuccessful and, following a siege lasting throughout the month of March 1746, Stapleton had to withdraw. Again, artillery – seized at Fort Augustus – was spiked and abandoned.

Jacobite operations at this time were certainly widely dispersed for, while these engagements were taking place, the Duke of Perth was directing efforts to mop up the remnants of Loudon's retreating army. Although Loudon himself eluded capture – being compelled to flee to Skye – many of

Culloden Moor.

his officers seemed only too anxious to surrender themselves and their men. In yet another theatre of operations, Murray attempted to take Blair Castle, and although he succeeded in securing the Pass of Killiecrankie, the approach of a relief party forced his eventual withdrawal. Despite all this activity and their apparent free run of the Highlands, the Jacobites failed to secure the safe arrival of more money, men and supplies from France, which were hijacked near Melness by the MacKays – serving to illustrate that not all the Highland clans were firmly behind the prince, who was usually to be seen amusing himself in Inverness.

The Road to Culloden

While Charles amused himself, Cumberland was busy amassing and training the most formidable army ever to be assembled against the Jacobites. Up to 8 April 1646, the Duke remained in Aberdeen, having arrived there from Perth on 27 February. Wisely, he ignored critics who argued that he should be moving more swiftly, for he had no intention of either marching his men into the ground or of mounting a premature, hastily prepared challenge.

When he finally did leave Aberdeen, it was with a well-supplied, confident army, supported by Royal Navy warships and transports sailing close inshore. Making up for any lost time, he arrived at Fochabars on the River Spey, just four days later. Waiting for him, on the west bank, was the Duke of Perth, commanding 2,000 men, surely intent on making a crossing of the Spey as difficult as possible. Bracing himself for heavy casualties, Cumberland ordered his men to ford the river in the early afternoon of 12 April. To his relief – and amazement – the Jacobites withdrew, and an opportunity to inflict limited damage on the Hanoverians was lost. Perth may have been acting under orders but, with little artillery support and the rest of the Jacobite army widely dispersed, there was, perhaps, something to be said for an orderly withdrawal. In fact, the retreat was not as orderly as Perth would have wished for, once across the Spey, Cumberland pressed on, to harass the Jacobite rearguard. At Nairn, for example, the Hanoverian vanguard arrived as the Jacobites were leaving.

Back in Inverness, frantic efforts were being made to muster all available Jacobite forces and the night of 14 April saw the bulk of the prince's army camped near Culloden House, on Drumossie Moor,[1] a tract of rough,

---

1   Later re-named Culloden Moor.

heavy, open ground immediately to the east. Lord George Murray did not relish the prospect of being brought to battle on Drumossie, which was far more suited to tactics involving artillery and concentrated rifle fire than to wild Highland charges. The prince, as with all the Stuarts, allowed his judgement to be swayed by flattery, and the prince's quartermaster, John William O'Sullivan, had quickly made himself a favourite by preying on the royal weakness. It was he who argued for the suitability of the moor as a field of battle, and nothing Murray could say would change Charles's mind on this score.

On the following day Murray proposed a night attack on the Hanoverian camp, an idea conceived through his anxiety to avoid, at all costs, a battle 'in so plain a feeld'. It was known that 15 April was Cumberland's 25th birthday and also that, regardless of the matter in hand, he intended to spend the day in celebration of this momentous occasion. The prince expressed his enthusiasm at the prospect of catching Cumberland unawares, and at 8.00 p.m. on 15th the Jacobites moved out in two columns, led by Charles and Murray respectively. The plan (in so far as there was one) involved a pincer movement culminating in an assault on the enemy camp at between 2.00 a.m. and 3.00 a.m., but the slow progress of the weary and hungry men meant that by 5.00 a.m., when the Hanoverians were already stirring, the Jacobites were still two miles away from their objective. There was nothing for it but to abandon the expedition and return to Drumossie where, on their arrival, most of the Highlanders threw themselves to the ground to sleep.

No sooner had they closed their eyes, it seemed, than Charles received news that Cumberland was on the move. Somehow, the exhausted Highlanders, 5,000 men, representing twenty-six clans, dragged themselves to their feet to form battle lines. Old rivalries resurfaced as the MacDonalds glumly made their way to the left of the front line, while Murray's Atholl Brigade took pride of place on the right. In between, from right to left, were the clans of Cameron, Stewarts of Appin, Frasers, Chattan, Farquharson, MacLachlan & Maclean, John Roy Stuart's Edinburgh Regiment and Chisholm. A second line, from right to left, comprised the clans of Ogilvy, Lewis Gordon, Glenbucket, the Duke of Perth's Regiment, Scots Royal and Brigadier Walter Stapleton's Irish Piquets. A third line, consisting mainly of light cavalry remained in the rear, ready to commence mopping-up operations when the Hanoverian lines collapsed – as they surely would do – in the face of the Highland infantry charge.

In fact, Cumberland's immaculately drilled troops looked most unlikely to break and run, deploying on the moor with speed and precision. The front line comprised six regiments of foot: Barrell's, Munro's, Campbell's, Price's, Cholmondeley's and Royal Scots, flanked by Kingston's Horse on the right and Lord Mark Kerr's dragoons on the left – Cobham's dragoons being split between the two commands. A second line also consisted of six regiments of foot: Sempill's, Bligh's, Conway's, Flemings, Howard's and Wolfe's with Pulteney's, Battereau's and Blakeney's in reserve. This deployment would be adjusted, according to needs, after the battle commenced, shortly after 1.00 p.m.

The Battle of Culloden

It is said that the first shot of the battle came from a Jacobite gun, and that it narrowly missed Cumberland – at 18 stone, a prominent target. If this is true, then the shot must have been a lucky one, for the Jacobite artillery, consisting of twelve guns positioned in the centre and on both flanks, were manned by inexperienced clansmen. Cumberland's artillery, under the competent command of Brevet-Colonel William Belford, comprised ten three-pounder guns, spread in pairs along the front line, with six mortars in two batteries of three to the rear. When Belford gave the order to return fire, the effect upon the tightly packed Highland ranks was devastating. Such was the accuracy of Belford's fire that the prince was forced to take up a position relatively out of harm's way, to the rear of his right flank.[2] This afforded him a poor view of the battlefield which was now enveloped in smoke, blowing into the Jacobite lines. For at least a quarter of an hour, the Highlanders remained immobile, moving only to close the gaps wrought in their ranks by Belford's cannon. Perhaps Charles thought that Cumberland would attack. If so, he was mistaken, for the Duke was naturally quite satisfied to see the Highlanders being cut to pieces at a distance. Under pressure from Murray, the prince finally gave the order for a Jacobite advance.

In preparation for the dreaded charge, Cumberland had broadened his front line with the addition of Pulteney's, while Battereau's were sent to strengthen the right flank of the second line. The extreme left of the battlefield was bordered by a wall, part stone and part turf, and Wolfe's were removed from the second line, to take up a position behind the wall, at right angles, so as to catch the advancing Highlanders in a cross-fire.

2 In the spring of 1996, on the 250th anniversary of the Battle of Culloden, a hitherto unknown contemporary sketch-map of the encounter came to light. Allegedly drawn by a French officer who fought with the Jacobites, the plan depicts the prince, in the early stages of the battle, leading from the front prior to a gradual retirement to the rear of his own lines.

When it came, however, the assault was not quite the fearsome spectacle of old. Normally, charging Highlanders might accelerate to a collision speed of 12 miles an hour, but the heavy ground slowed them up. In addition, the advance was uneven, with the centre leading off – possibly before the order was given – and the Atholl Brigade following up as soon as orders were received. Still sulking because the Atholl Brigade had taken what they believed was their rightful position, and understandably confused about what, if anything, they should be doing, the MacDonalds on the left did not charge at all. By this time, Belford's guns were being loaded with grapeshot – lead balls, nails and jagged metal – to cause even greater carnage within the Highland ranks. To complete the picture, as they drew closer to the Hanoverian lines, the Highlanders were also absorbing concentrated musket fire.

When contact was made, Barrell's and part of Munro's bore the brunt of the attackers' rage. The wall forced the Atholl Brigade to the left, while the Highland centre, turned off-course either by the nature of the terrain or the murderous fire from the Hanoverian ranks, swung in to the right. The resulting congestion added to the slaughter, the cross-fire from Wolfe's proving particularly effective, but the surviving Highlanders managed to force their way through to Sempill's, who stood their ground, putting into practice a new stratagem whereby each man used his bayonet on the attacker to his left, thereby aiming for the unshielded portion of his body. With Barrell's and Munro's to their rear and Sempill's to their front, many Highlanders who had fought their way into the Hanoverian lines found it doubly hard to fight their way out.

Had the Jacobite charge been coordinated – and launched immediately – then Cumberland might have been hard pressed to contain it. However, the duke's artillery had torn the heart out of the Highland attack. In addition, the overall commitment of the clans from the centre to the left of the Jacobite front line left much to be desired. Most of the Farquharsons, together with John Roy Stewart's – the latter not possessing swords – never came to grips with the enemy, taking flight to leave the MacDonalds exposed on both flanks. In an attempt to draw Pulteney's and the Royal Scots out into the open by taunting them, MacDonald of Keppoch led a series of swift dashes half way down the field, which succeeded only in drawing more deadly fire. Finally, when they were passed by the clans of the centre and right in full retreat, they too turned and ran. It was left largely to Keppoch, his brother, Donald, and a handful of officers to salvage a little honour by running on to their deaths.

With most of the Highlanders in flight, Cumberland now unleashed his cavalry. On the right, Kingston's and Cobham's rode out in pursuit of the MacDonalds, whose withdrawal was partially covered by a courageous stand made by the Irish Piquets. On the right, Murray could be seen trying

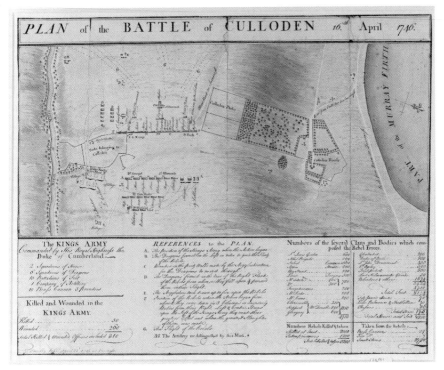

Thomas Sandby's Plan of the Battle of Culloden. (The Royal Collection 1996, HM The Queen)

to turn the tide by leading forward the only regiments remaining intact: Gordon's and the Royal Scots, but it was a forlorn hope. The key to the outcome of the fighting on this wing was proving to be the wall, behind which a regiment of Campbell's Argyll Militia had stationed itself. Cumberland never really trusted the Campbells who were, after all, clansmen and in most respects indistinguishable from his Jacobite enemies. But they did him good service on that day, maintaining a heavy cross-fire and making a breach in the wall to allow the passage of Kerr's and Cobham's horse. As Stapleton's Irish Piquets had blunted the pursuit on the right, so Balmerino's and Elcho's and Fitzjames's horse now temporarily delayed Kerr's and Cobham's. And, like MacDonald of Keppoch, Lord Strathallan chose an honourable death by leading a hopeless charge on Cobham's.

The battle, which lasted less than one hour, was now all but over, enabling Cumberland to initiate a systematic programme of bloody revenge, earning himself, in the process, the additional title of The Butcher.

The Aftermath

The contribution to the battle of Prince Charles Edward was limited to the belated encouragement of individual Highlanders as they fled the moor. As if unable to accept defeat, he was led away, dazed and confused, while the survivors of the Jacobite right wing, under Murray's skilful management, retreated to the River Nairn. So disciplined was the withdrawal that the victors felt safer in wreaking vengeance on the disorganized left wing and upon the wounded.

Only a century before, during the English Civil War, opposing generals had vied with one another for the honour of making provision for the wounded. The aftermath of Culloden was very different, for this was total war, in which the victorious regime ruthlessly pursued its concept of a 'final solution' to the Highland problem. As the Hanoverian infantry regiments advanced to take possession of the field, the wounded Highlanders were despatched with bayonet thrusts. General Henry Hawley's dragoons, engaged in cutting down Highlanders and civilians alike who were fleeing down the narrow lanes leading to Inverness, missed the moment of triumph.

Cumberland's pause was only a short one, for he was soon marching on Inverness, passing the night of 16 April in a house used by the prince. The following day, letting it be known that the Jacobite army had been acting under orders to give no quarter to the enemy – an unfounded rumour – he instructed his men to scour the countryside for survivors. Some of the wounded who had managed to hide in the sparse undergrowth of the moor eluded detection for three or four days before being run-through, shot or clubbed to death. Mass executions took place in the surrounding cottages and farm buildings where groups of wounded fugitives had sought refuge. Some of the most diligent executioners were Lowland Scots, who rivalled the English in the contempt they felt for their Highland countrymen. By the end of May, the newly garrisoned forts were serving as bases for army patrols to extend to the Highland glens the policy of burning, looting and killing.

On the battlefield itself, at least 1,000 Highlanders lost their lives – against 50 Hanoverians – and, despite the carnage following the battle, almost 3,500 were taken prisoner and 120 'lawfully' executed. A handful, including Lords Balmerino and Kilmarnock, were beheaded, while the rest suffered the traditional traitor's death of hanging, drawing and quartering. A total of 936 were transported as slave labour to the Americas.

In the longer term, persecution of all Highlanders, whether or not they were active Jacobite supporters, continued. It is to be doubted whether Disarming Acts were any more successful than they had been in the past in encouraging the clans to surrender their weapons, but the new legislation, extended to include a ban on Highland dress, certainly helped to destroy Highland culture and identity. Another measure aimed at destruction of the clan system was the Heritable Jurisdictions Act of 1747 which abolished courts of regality, including those of the clan chiefs, so reducing their feudal powers over man and beast.

Charles remained at large in the west for several months, before taking a French ship for the continent. That he was able to evade capture for so long, with a price of £30,000 on his head, says much for the loyalty of his Highland supporters. It had been hoped, initially, that the remnants of his defeated army would regroup until, with uncharacteristic decisiveness, the prince issued the statement: 'Let every man seek his own safety the best way he can.' As far as he was concerned, the game was over, his main preoccupation from then on being to save his own skin regardless of the risks incurred by those who gave him shelter. Lord George Murray escaped abroad to spend his days travelling in Europe. The paths of the prince and his brilliant general were never to cross again, even though Charles also resumed an itinerant lifestyle. To the end, he blamed Murray for the failure of the '45 which is further proof, if any were needed, that he was most assuredly 'of the family'.

The Jacobite movement – and Charles's optimism – survived Culloden, as demonstrated in the Elibank Plot of 1749–53, a protracted scheme aimed at the assassination of George II and the proclamation of Charles Edward as regent. Although the plotters were discovered, canvassing of the Highland clans suggested that some were ready to pledge their support yet again. In truth, however, Charles had already become the 'Bonnie Prince Charlie' of legend, a romantic, heroic figure worthy of the society which was sacrificed on the altar of his cause.

The Walk

Distance: 4 miles (6.44 km)

Begin at the National Trust for Scotland Visitor Centre (Pathfinder 177–745451) (Point A). Complete with splendid displays, auditorium, bookshop and refreshment facilities, the centre must rank as one of Britain's premier battlefield attractions. As with Sheriffmuir, much of the battle ground was planted with conifers. In 1980, however, 108 acres were purchased from the Forestry Commission and cleared. Further generous donations of land followed. The only potential problem is that one does tend

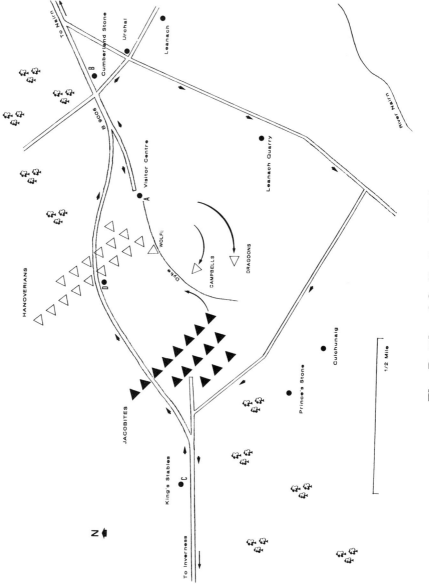

The Battle of Culloden, 1746

to interpret the battle within the confines of the Trust's property boundaries, whereas key actions took place over a somewhat wider area.

For this reason, it is suggested that the Visitor Centre marks the conclusion, rather than the start, of a more extensive exploration. Therefore, leaving the Visitor Centre, walk back towards the Culloden Moor Inn. At the other side of the crossroads is the 'Cumberland Stone' (Pathfinder 177–750453) (Point B), marking the spot from where the Duke of Cumberland is said to have viewed the action and/or had lunch afterwards. Although the duke must have been constantly on the move, the point may provide a useful marker for the immediate rear of the Hanoverian lines.

Return to the crossroads and turn left. At the next crossroads – in the hamlet of Urchal – turn right. The manoeuvres on the extreme left of the Hanoverian lines, involving the Campbell irregulars and the dragoons took place at a point mid-way between this road and the Visitor Centre. Continue walking, past the quarry, and take the track on the right (Pathfinder 177–746444) leading to Culchunaig. In the field to the left, immediately beyond Culchunaig, is the 'Prince's Stone' (Pathfinder 177–737444), denoting Prince Charles Edward's position and, perhaps, the extreme right of the Jacobite lines.

Continue walking – along a route which would have taken one through the rear of the Jacobite lines – to the B9006 and turn to the left. A little way up on the right-hand side is King's Stables Cottage (Pathfinder 177–734448) (Point C), occupying a site which housed Hanoverian dragoons in the aftermath of the battle. Return along the B9006, which runs across the battlefield, and thence back to the Visitor Centre.

After a viewing of the film of the Culloden campaign, it is a simple matter, with the aid of the superlative NTS guidebook, to explore the 'interior' of the battlefield. Although the walls, which played such an important part in the battle, no longer exist, their course may be taken to correspond, very roughly, with the present-day field boundaries – allowing, of course, for the protuberance restricting the advance of the Jacobite right wing. A series of paths enable one to make a circular tour of the central area, with its numerous memorial stones. To help visualize the true extent of the arena, one should stand at the north-east corner of the rectangular path (Pathfinder 177–743453) (Point D). The Hanoverian line extended away to the north, as far as, and possibly beyond, Hollybush (Pathfinder 177–741455.) Before leaving the Visitor Centre, one should visit Old Leanach Cottage, adjacent to the Visitor Centre (a function which the cottage performed prior to the construction of its replacement). In outhouses belonging to the cottage, some thirty wounded Highlanders were burned alive by the Hanoverian search parties which roamed the battlefield and its environs for days afterwards.

Despite the well-groomed appearance of the NTS site, many people have remarked on the sense of sadness which pervades Culloden, and there have been many sightings of apparitions, including ghostly re-enactments of the battle.

Further Explorations

The woodland and the railway line combined have left Culloden House (Pathfinder 177–721465) languishing in splendid isolation. At the time of both the '15 and the '45, it was home to Duncan Forbes, Lord President of the Court of Session and formidable opponent of the Jacobites. The present late eighteenth-century building, now used as a hotel, replaced the lord president's castellated mansion house which was destroyed by fire. Not surprisingly, perhaps, the house is said to be haunted by the ghost of Prince Charles Edward.

To the north, running along the Moray Firth coastline is an old (post-Wade) military road, the B9030, linking Inverness with Fort George (Landranger 27–7652). Fort George (Landranger 27–7756) is probably the best example of an eighteenth-century artillery fortification in Europe. Building began in 1748 and took twenty years to complete, at a cost of £160,000. It is a simple matter for twentieth-century commentators to consign post '45 Jacobitism to the footnotes of history. At the time, however, the prospect of further Highland rebellions could by no means be discounted, and so no expense was spared in the drive for greater security. Over 2,000 men could be quartered on the fort's 15-acre site which, as a first line of defence, has a substantial V-shaped outwork or ravelin, to keep attackers at bay. Still used by the military, Fort George has changed little in the past two centuries.

To the south-east of the battlefield beyond the River Nairn are the Clava Cairns (Pathfinder 177–757445), three burial chambers, dating from 2000 BC, surrounded by standing stones. On-site interpretation boards describe the grouping, which one may visit during the suggested walk by taking the Leanach road to the south of the Culloden Visitor Centre.

To the west, reaching out tentatively towards Culloden is Inverness, host to four famous castles. The Pictish King Brude may have held court in a castle on Craig Phadrig (Pathfinder 177–640453) in the sixth century, while one of the preferred sites for Macbeth's castle is the high ground on Auldcastle Road (Pathfinder 177–675456). Here, a timber structure was eventually replaced with a stone castle overlooking the River Ness on Castle Hill (Pathfinder 177–667451) which, in turn, was destroyed – this time by King Robert I during the Wars of Independence. Rebuilt and strengthened at intervals over successive centuries, it was besieged by Montrose in 1645 and extended by General Wade. Rechristened 'Fort George', the castle was held by the Hanoverians until February 1746, when the garrison commander, Major Grant, surrendered to the besieging Jacobite army. Mines were laid under all the bastions and the fort completely gutted. The present-day castle dates from 1834. The fourth major fortification was The Citadel built at the mouth of the Ness (Pathfinder 177–665464) during 1652–5. Known more colloquially as 'Oliver's Fort', the star-shaped structure could house a garrison of 1,000. Following the Restoration, orders were issued to demolish it. A single tower, known as 'Cromwell's Tower' has survived.

Friar's Lane, by the footbridge (Pathfinder 177–665455) is the site of a thirteenth-century Dominican monastery, demolished in order to provide building materials for The Citadel. An adjacent graveyard contains the tomb of Alexander Stewart, self-constituted Earl of Mar, victor of the Battle of Reid Harlaw (24 July 1411), an encounter between Stewart and his cousin, Donald, 2nd Lord of the Isles, which is popularly believed to have cemented the growing antagonism between Highlanders and Lowlanders, establishing once and for all that Scotland was – and remains – a country of two quite distinct nations.

Further Information

The battlefield of Culloden is located on the B9006 which links Nairn with Inverness. The National Trust for Scotland Visitor Centre, 5 miles east of Inverness, is well signposted. Inverness is also the rail head for which travellers by train should aim. An hourly Bluebird bus from Inverness includes Culloden on a route which also takes in Elgin, Forres, Nairn and Aberdeen. (Telephone 01224–212266 for further information.)

The battlefield site is open all year. For details of the varying opening times of the Visitor Centre, shop and site restaurant, call the Resident Property Manager on 01463–790607. For additional tourist information, and a copy of *On The Move: Around Inverness, Loch Ness and Nairn*, contact the Inverness Tourist Information Centre, Castle Wynd, Inverness IV2 3BJ (telephone 01463 234353). Prospective visitors to Fort George (in the care of Historic Scotland) should telephone 01667–462777 for information regarding access. Admission information relating to Inverness Castle may be obtained by telephoning 01463–243363.

Only one Ordnance Survey Pathfinder is required: No. 177. The relevant Landranger map is No. 27. Identification of books for further reading presents no problem. The modern 'classic' is John Prebble's *Culloden*. It is difficult to believe that this book, which is valuable for its detailed coverage of the battle's aftermath, was written thirty-five years ago, in 1961. Jeremy Black's *Culloden and the '45*, on the other hand, concentrates on the events leading up to the battle. Sir Charles Petrie's *The Jacobite Movement, the Last Phase*, has withstood the test of time, while *Battles of the '45* by Katherine Tomasson and Francis Buist contains a very readable account. Neither should one ignore two excellent HMSO publications, Robert Woosnam-Savage's *1745: Charles Edward Stuart and the Jacobites* and Michael Hook and Walter Ross's *The Forty-Five*. The National Trust for Scotland's own immaculately produced booklet, *Culloden*, is an essential companion for an exploration of the battlefield.

12
RAF EAST FORTUNE
1940–6

Introduction

The Battle of Culloden in 1746 effectively put an end to warfare between England and Scotland. By this time, the days of fierce border warfare were long gone by, and the Scottish Lowlands were completely 'pacified'. As remarked elsewhere, many Lowlanders fought with the English at Culloden, going on to play a vigorous part in the bloody pursuit which followed. With the ensuing destruction of the Highlanders' way of life, the clans, too, were brought to heel.

When England declared war – in both 1914 and 1939 – she did so on the behalf of a vast Empire, dragging into both conflicts people inhabiting up to one quarter of the earth's surface, including Scotland. Far from constituting a part of this Empire, it might be argued that the Scots made an invaluable contribution to its creation. In the latter part of the eighteenth century, within living memory of Culloden, for example, Scots were making their mark in British India. During the nineteenth century, Lords Dalhousie and Elgin would occupy the highest office in India – that of governor-general – while, militarily, the Raj was reliant upon Scottish soldiers for keeping intact the jewel in the crown. Sir Colin Campbell, for example, served in the Napoleonic Wars and in the Crimea before going on to India as commander-in-chief of the army and raising the siege of Lucknow.

The year 1740 had witnessed the creation of the 'Black Watch', the first Highland regiment in the British Army, which had developed from a number of independent companies of Highlanders, formed to support the English regulars in the preservation of law and order. However, it was to the industrial cities of Scotland that the recruiting officers increasingly turned in their search for manpower. The slum population of the major towns and cities had been much expanded by the exodus from the Highlands as a result of the 'Highland Clearances'. Many Highlanders emigrated – albeit to

America in preference to the colonies – but the less adventurous, in the hopeless quest for employment, drifted into the industrial areas where the maladies born of overcrowding added to their misfortunes. Occasionally, recruitment would take place at the source of discontent – the Western Isles suffering particularly heavy losses per head of population in conflicts as diverse as the Napoleonic Wars and the First World War. More often than not, however, the tenements of Dundee, Glasgow and the Clyde supplied victims for the killing fields of Europe and the farthest outposts of Empire.

On Sunday 3 September 1939, when the *Edinburgh Evening News* informed its readers that Britain was at war, the editor added the words: 'Premier Tells the Nation by Radio'. The 'Nation' was no longer Scotland, but Britain. A tiny paragraph in the same edition referred to emergency parliamentary legislation in respect of Northern Ireland, for 'defence purposes'. Was there anyone then living in Scotland, whose great grandparents, long dead, would have remembered the time when the English government would have entertained similar fears in respect of Scottish loyalties? Fortunately for unity, the first U-boat casualty of the conflict was a Glasgow liner, the *Athenia*. The stories of the survivors, who were taken to Greenock, helped to make up the minds of many doubting Scots.

The Nazi perception of Anglo-Scottish unity was somewhat different. In 1941, Hitler's deputy, Rudolf Hess, tried to negotiate a meeting with English officials on neutral ground. In the end, he flew his ME 110 to Scotland, hoping to parachute onto the Duke of Hamilton's estate.[1] Having no wish to communicate with Churchill, Hess may have considered Hamilton's seat, Dungavel House, sufficiently remote from the seat of government to lessen the risk of immediate arrest. In fact, he wanted Hamilton to head a peace mission with a view to reaching an amicable agreement with Germany, and it is interesting that, in his eyes at least, Scotland still had the potential to challenge Westminster in time of war. Unfortunately for the deputy führer, the duke was not at home.

The Road to East Fortune

One of the most intriguing aspects of the development of flying machines concerns the appearance of the airship, or 'dirigible'. For a time, it looked as though the future of passenger air travel rested with the airship – an idea for

---

1 Hess had hoped to engineer a meeting with the duke through a mutual friend, Albrecht Haushofer.

A Beaufighter of RAF Coastal Command. (Imperial War Museum)

which there is qualified support even today.[2] Advances in aerospace technology, as in many other areas of human endeavour, have been accelerated by the demands of war, and the course of events at East Fortune during the First World War illustrate both the early rivalry between airship and aeroplane, and the rapid progress which could be made when the national survival was at stake.

In 1914, the Germans, appreciating the military potential of the airship, embarked on a considerable construction programme, and within a few months, 'zeppelins' were making feared raids over English towns and cities – including Edinburgh. To combat the latter threat, an airfield was established at East Fortune, but the rickety little Sopwith Sea Scout aeroplanes proved unequal to the task of effectively challenging the high-flying dirigibles.

In fact, zeppelins were only one half of the problem, for German submarines were also operating in the Firth of Forth. It was found that airships, armed with machine guns and carrying bomb loads of 400lb, were

---

[2]   Britain, the United States of America, Germany, Russia and Canada all currently (1996) have ambitious airship construction plans in hand.

a more efficient deterrent than aeroplanes in dealing with – or at least in spotting – the U-Boats, and East Fortune became a Royal Naval Air Service station specializing in coastal patrol duties. The British 'North Sea Class' airships were small, non-rigid craft – i.e. with limp bags, which gave rise to the term 'blimps'.

However, with their head start, the Germans continued to improve and perfect their own zeppelins with comparative ease. Thus, there were no immediate benefits when one of the famous Sopwith Pup aeroplanes, which arrived at East Fortune in 1917, achieved a height of 19,000 feet, for, by this time, the zeppelins were able to operate at a staggering 25,000 feet.

Strangely enough for those pioneer days of flying, aircraft were already taking off from the decks of ships, and from the early part of 1917, East Fortune was used as a base for such operations. On 1 April 1918, with the amalgamation of the Royal Naval Air Service and the Royal Flying Corps, the Royal Air Force came into being. As an RAF station, East Fortune served as a base for the development of ambitious plans to bomb the German fleet in port. The objective was to be achieved by having a squadron of Sopwith Cuckoos fitted with torpedoes. They would then be transported to within striking range by HMS *Argus*. Considerable training was involved, and the Cuckoos, which had their torpedoes fitted on the beach at Dunbar, made practice runs along the coast. Problems experienced with the Cuckoos' engines led to further, unscheduled delays so that the month of October 1918 was well advanced before a state of anything approaching readiness was achieved. The scheme was finally scuppered, not by logistical difficulties, but by the end of the war itself, with the signing of the Armistice on 11 November 1918.

Momentarily, it looked as though RAF East Fortune might have a future, at least as an airship base. During the final months of the war, two rigid airships – the R24 and the R29 – had been accommodated here. Immediately after the war, in 1919, it was decided that the giant R34 should use East Fortune as the starting point for her attempt to make the first east–west crossing of the Atlantic. Alcock and Brown had flown their Vickers-Vimy across the Atlantic on 14 June 1919, but the very first crossing had been made in May by a US Navy seaplane, skippered by Lieutenant-Commander A.C. Read – an achievement which does not seem to have carried much weight because a refuelling stop at the Azores had been built in to the flight plan. The projected east–west crossing was expected to be difficult in that the R34 would be struggling against the same westerly winds which had helped Alcock and Brown. On 2 July, she embarked on the voyage that would set two records: the first east–west Atlantic crossing and the world's longest endurance time of 108 hours and 12 minutes. More records were broken on the return trip, but instead of reappearing at East Fortune, the R34 was diverted to Pulham. This was a blow from which East Fortune failed to recover, and although it remained nominally active for a few more months, operations officially ceased in 1920, after which only essential care and maintenance work was carried out.

RAF East Fortune 1940–6

East Fortune was one of several First World War airfields which were given a new lease of life with the onset of the Second World War. In 1918, there had been 301 airfields – a number which, within six years, had been reduced to twenty-seven. This situation changed during the mid–1930s, when the fear of a rapidly re-arming Nazi Germany led to the establishment of 100 new airfields.

The inter-war years had witnessed the demise of the airship, a series of disasters having demonstrated that the future of air travel – in times of both war and peace – lay with the aeroplane. The British R101 had crashed in flames over France in 1930, the German *Hindenburg* following suit at Lakehurst in America, in 1937. During the First World War, in its airship days, there had been primitive domestic facilities at East Fortune, consisting of a number of wooden huts situated at the northern end of the airfield. This portion of the site underwent conversion to a sanatorium for sufferers of tuberculosis – at the time, a widespread, incurable disease. In 1940, however, when it was decided to resurrect East Fortune as a satellite station for RAF Drem, the premises were requisitioned.

Three runways, of hardcore with a tarmac dressing, were constructed. These were of a standard width of 50 yards, and of three lengths: 1,710, 1,560 and 1,100 yards. There were three Callender Hamilton aircraft hangars and a 'T2' hangar. Because it could be erected speedily, the latter type, built by the Tee-Side Bridge & Engineering Company, became the most popular during the war years. All four of East Fortune's main hangars have survived. The half-dozen small 'Over Blister' hangars which were also added, have not stood the test of time.

In addition to the main airfield site, a total of thirteen dispersed domestic sites were built, with the aim of accommodating a maximum of 1,501 RAF and 704 WAAF personnel. All were situated to the south of the airfield, and only two have survived the ravages of peacetime.

It was not until June 1941 that RAF East Fortune's war began in earnest, with the arrival of Operational Training Unit 60. Geared to the training of night fighter crews, the unit comprised an assortment of Blenheims, Oxfords, Defiants and Miles Masters. Later that year, this unwieldy mix was reduced to Blenheims and Beaufighters. Unlike the other branches of the armed services, however, the RAF seems to have been committed to a continuous process of reorganization – a wonderful method, as Caius Petronius (AD 66) pointed out, for creating the illusion of progress. And so, in November 1942, the excellent 60 Operational Training Unit was reorganized into 132 OTU, under the auspices of Coastal Command. To be fair, the importance of Coastal Command's contribution to the war effort made the transfer of units inevitable. At first, its role had been limited to one of aerial reconnaissance, but, as time went on, U-boat search and destroy operations became of increasing importance. The purpose of 132 OTU was to train crews in such strike operations.

Initially, of course, it had been presumed that RAF East Fortune would serve the same purpose as the RFC base during the First World War – i.e. to provide added protection to the towns of East Lothian and, in particular, Edinburgh. As it happened, Edinburgh did not suffer from Luftwaffe air raids to the extent which had been anticipated. During the whole of the war, there were only fourteen bombing raids on the city. Aberdeen had thirty-four raids, while Clydebank, under constant bombardment soaked up 1,329 tons of high explosive. For this reason also, East Fortune's role was bound to develop.

From April 1944, De Havilland Mosquitos, known as 'Wooden Wonders' by virtue of their efficiency, began replacing the Beaufighters, and during 1945, as the war finally drew to a close, Mosquito VIs formed the basis of East Fortune's armoury.

The Aftermath

As with so many wartime airfields, it seemed that no sooner had RAF East Fortune got into its stride – with over thirty Mosquito VIs on its strength – than the war ended. Some stations shut down almost immediately, but East Fortune's withdrawal from active service was more gradual, OTU 132 not being disbanded until May 1946 – with the ultimate return of the northern section of the main airfield site to the Sanatorium Board.

In 1950, there was a brief flurry of activity when, with the onset of the Cold War, East Fortune was earmarked for the USAF. Several Second World War airfields took on a new lease of life in this period, with some going on to furnish accommodation for Thor missiles. Such was the level of reconstruction which would have been required at East Fortune that plans never went ahead.

For a period in 1961, East Fortune became Edinburgh Airport, while runway work was undertaken at Turnhouse, and it seems remarkable that this remote airfield was able to handle all the city's air traffic during the busy summer months. Like the air crews which had spent the war years there, East Fortune seemed to have developed a will to survive against all the odds for, in 1973, a decision was taken to develop a portion of the main airfield site as a Museum of Flight, which eventually opened two years later.

It would be a pity if conservation of the airfield, an important part of the nation's heritage, were to be limited to the museum compound. Although light aircraft still make use of the runways, the roar of engines within recent years has emanated from organized motorcycle racing, as well as from private cars attending regular open air markets. The appearance of 'For Sale' signs at the hospital end constitute, perhaps, an ominous hint of things to come.

As far as the air war in general was concerned, enemy bombing had destroyed thousands of homes. Clydebank took the lion's share, with Greenock reduced to rubble. However, it has to be admitted that there were long-term benefits, with much-needed rebuilding programmes being forced upon many communities. Other beneficial side-effects of the air war arose as a result of the evacuation programme. The list of items with which mothers had to supply the evacuees was quite basic, and included a warm coat, a change of underclothes, night attire and washing kit. It soon became apparent that to many children, especially those from the Glasgow tenements, coats, a change of underwear, pyjamas and face cloths were luxuries which their families could not afford to provide. In addition, there was evidence of much neglect in matters of personal hygiene.

The post-war Labour government did its best to alleviate urban poverty and to provide decent housing. However Nationalist sentiment, forever simmering beneath the surface, was destined to develop slowly but surely into an influential political force. In 1944 an SNP candidate, who had opposed conscription in Scotland, had come very near to winning a by-election in Kirkaldy, a clear indication of a feeling that Scotland should not be called upon to help England fight wars in which she became embroiled. With the exception of the immediate post-war Atlee administration, the interest in Scottish affairs of all British governments since 1945 has been regulated by the extent to which their survival has been dependent upon the support of the Scottish electorate. It would come as no surprise, therefore, to Robert the Bruce if he were to learn that six centuries after Bannockburn, the Nationalists are, once more, turning to Europe for support in their quest for independence.

The Walk

Distance: 6 miles (9.66 km)

Begin at the Museum of Flight, based at East Fortune's main airfield site (Pathfinder 408–552783) (Point A). Car parking is provided by the main exhibition hangar (Pathfinder 408–554784), which makes for a good starting point. This T2 hangar, constructed with thirty-two bays, is now

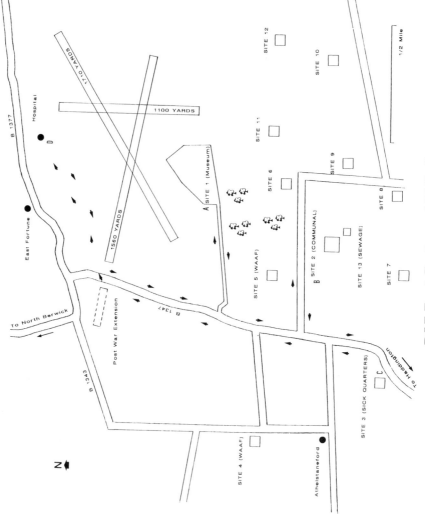

RAF East Fortune 1940–6

connected to an annexe – once a separate building – housing a café and shop, where some excellent publications are on sale. As far as the Second World War is concerned, the main hangar's exhibits are of the most interest. The two aircraft with which one will be most familiar are the Supermarine Spitfire and the Messerschmitt Me 163. Despite the undoubted strengths of the former, surviving Spitfire pilots do recall that they often found themselves both outmanoeuvred and outgunned by the Messerschmitts.

The oldest exhibit is Pilcher's 'Hawk' glider. Percy Pilcher was a British aviation pioneer who, but for his premature death in a flying accident, might well have beaten the Wright Brothers in the race to stage the first powered flight.

From the main hangar, proceed to the storage hangar, like the remaining two hangars, a Callender Hamilton, with exhibits which include a 1960s Blackburn Buccaneer jet aircraft. The path between the storage hangar and the aerospace hangar is bordered by various stores and workshop buildings, while the aerospace hangar itself houses examples of naval aircraft from the 1950s as well as two Soviet MIG Jets. In addition, there is a section relating to space flight, which includes the celebrated Blue Streak, epitomizing Britain's efforts to keep pace in the escalating worldwide arms race of the 1950s. The exterior compound contains a De Havilland Comet. The embodiment of yet another doomed British bid for supremacy in an ever competitive world, the Comet operated the first jet airliner service. Unfortunately, the explosion in

Dispersed Site No. 3, RAF East Fortune.

mid-air of two Comets during the first few months of 1954 led to a loss of confidence from which the British aviation industry was slow to recover.

Take the path to the rear of the compound and walk down to the access road via the two stores buildings. Leave the main site, on foot, and walk down to the B1347 and turn to the left. Take the first turning on the left for Home Farm and Gilmerton House, continuing as far as Communal Site No. 2 (Pathfinder 408–547775) (Point B) which contains surviving site buildings improvised and modified for farming purposes. Of particular interest here is the dining room (Pathfinder 408–548775) and the games room (Pathfinder 408–548773), a building which, among other things, also contained the education centre and the chaplain's office.

Returning to the B1347, turn to the left and walk as far as Site No. 3 (Pathfinder 408–539770) (Point C) which lies just beyond the Athelstaneford turn-off. Here, the road seems to bend more sharply than suggested on the Ordnance Survey map, so a little care is needed. The surviving buildings, very well preserved, once acted as sick quarters but, again, have been converted for farm use. The group of three to the rear, with connecting corridors still intact, contained twenty-four beds for RAF and WAAF personnel. The building standing alone to the fore doubled as an ambulance garage and mortuary.

It is now necessary to retrace one's steps, walking past the museum entrance and on towards East Fortune. The airfield runways come into view to the right, at the end of the plantation. By walking around the perimeter road – across part of the area occupied by the First World War airfield – one can view the sanatorium site (Point D). The sergeants' mess and sick quarters (crash ward) (Pathfinder 408–554794) were modified after the war to form part of the sanatorium, and one of three sergeants' quarters timber-built huts has survived (Pathfinder 408–553793). After viewing, return to the road and walk back to the museum.[3]

Further Explorations

East Fortune may be visited as part of a wider exploration of the rugged North Berwick coast, for which Pathfinder 408 is recommended. An interesting feature of the coastline is the series of small islands, little more

---

3 The suggested walk takes account of the better preserved sites only, and it is hoped that visitors will wish to explore the area more fully.

than outcrops of rock, punctuating the southern reaches of the Firth of Forth. The northernmost of these is Bass Rock (Pathfinder 408–602874). Today, Bass Rock is renowned for its gannet colonies, but in the eighth century, it was home to the Celtic missionary, Saint Baldred, as evinced by the remains of a sixteenth-century chapel dedicated to his memory. Also prominent, on the south side, are the remains of a fifteenth-century castle. The proven military potential of the site was recognized by Sir William Brereton in 1634. Brereton became a successful Roundhead commander during the English Civil War, and he must have recalled his shrewd assessment when, sixteen years after his visit, the Royalists secured Bass as a base for naval operations in the Firth of Forth. In 1671, the castle became a prison for political prisoners, and a bleak existence it must have been for both the inmates and their keepers. In 1691, four Jacobite prisoners succeeded in taking control of the fortress while most of the garrison was engaged in the landing of supplies. Subsequently reinforced, the party held out for nearly three years. Tiring of their attacks on shipping and of their lightning coastal raids, the authorities eventually allowed them very favourable terms of surrender.

The town of North Berwick (Pathfinder 408–555855) is infamous for its witchcraft trials of the 1590s. A widespread belief in witchcraft was often exploited by European rulers for the attainment of political ends. And so, James VI claimed that a coven (allegedly headed by the Earl of Bothwell) was responsible for conjuring up a storm off Bass Rock, and almost wrecking the ship carrying James and his new queen, Anne of Denmark. The trials themselves took place in the old church of St Andrew's, the remains of which may be seen (Pathfinder 408–555856). Immediately to the south of the town is North Berwick Law (Pathfinder 408–556843), capped by an Iron Age Hill Fort, an outstanding vantage point.

The area also contains the remains of several medieval fortresses. Waughton Castle (Pathfinder 408–568809) was recognized as a strategic stronghold in the sixteenth century and saw action on more than one occasion, while Fenton Tower (Pathfinder 408–544821) is an excellent example of a sixteenth-century fortified house. However, the most spectacular fortress in the locality is Tantallon Castle (Pathfinder 408–597851). Although a castle has occupied the rocky promontory since the twelfth century, the surviving curtain wall, 50 feet high and 12 feet thick, dates from about 1350, shortly after which the Douglas family took possession. Both James IV (1491) and James V (1528) laid siege to the castle, but were unable to take it by force. In 1651, garrisoned by Royalist troops, it was still a tough nut to crack, and only after a twelve-day bombardment by heavy cannon did it fall to General Monck.

Dirleton Castle (Pathfinder 408–516839) is perhaps the most picturesque castle in the district. The earliest portion, a cluster of towers, dates from the early thirteenth century. In 1298, it was besieged and eventually taken by the English, who maintained a garrison there until 1311, when King Robert I won it back. Robert, who vandalized several castles in the interests of national security, demolished much of the original structure. Rebuilding work carried out in the fourteenth and fifteenth centuries suffered severe damage in 1650 when the castle, held for the Royalists, fell to an assault by Monck and Lambert, whose reputations were somewhat tarnished by the decision to execute several of the defenders.

To the south of Dirleton is Drem and, in particular, the site of the wartime airfield (Pathfinder 408–506814). Like East Fortune, it was functional during the First World War. In the opening weeks of the Second World War, a fighter from Drem shot down one of the first enemy aircraft flying over Britain, and the station also gave its name to a runway lighting system. Unusually for such a busy station, Drem's grass landing strips were never replaced with concrete runways. As a result, little has survived outside the main airfield site.

Drem was closed in 1946 and although only fifty years have elapsed, the war to which it belongs now seems as remote as many an earlier conflict. The RAF Spitfire pilots, flying to victory in the Battle of Britain, have taken their places alongside 'Johnnie' Cope's English army en route to defeat at Prestonpans, Cromwell's Roundheads triumphant at Dunbar, the Duke of Somerset's men-at-arms on the road to Pinkie and Edward II's English knights riding to their deaths at Bannockburn.

Further Information

East Fortune lies directly off the A1, on the B1347, to the north-east of Haddington. The Museum of Flight entrance (concealed) is almost opposite Athelmead (Pathfinder 408–543782). The branch railway line, which once connected Haddington with Edinburgh, has been dismantled and turned into a walking/cycling track. East Fortune, on the main Edinburgh–London (King's Cross) line, once had its own railway station (Pathfinder 408–558796), but the nearest station is now at Drem, on the Edinburgh–North Berwick line. From Drem, a pleasant walk of 2 miles, via Appin, will take one to the Museum of Flight. For details of regular bus services between Haddington and East Linton, call 0131–654707.

The Museum of Flight enjoys only a short season (April to September), although it is open between 10.30 a.m. and 4.30 p.m. for seven days a week during these months. Current information concerning opening times and entry fees may be obtained by telephoning 01620–880308. Information about the surrounding area is available in the tourist publications recommended elsewhere in this book: *East Lothian Holiday Guide* and *East Lothian Visitor Attractions and Activities*, available from the Tourist Information Centre, Quality Street, North Berwick (telephone 01620–892197) or The Tourist Information Centre, Pencraig, Haddington (telephone 01620–860063).

For background reading, David J. Smith's *Action Stations Vol 7: Military Airfields of Scotland, the North-East and Northern Ireland* is recommended, together with the same author's *Britain's Military Airfields 1939–45*. A National Museums of Scotland booklet entitled *Museum of Flight* available from the Museum of Flight, provides specific information about flying activities at East Fortune over the years.

FURTHER READING

Place of publication given only if outside London.

General background reading:

Clough, Monica, *The Field of Thistles: Scotland's Past & Scotland's People* (MacDonald, Edinburgh, 1983)

Mackie, J.D., *A History of Scotland* (Penguin Books Ltd, Harmondsworth, 1978)

Maclean, Fitzroy, *A Concise History of Scotland* (Thames & Hudson, 1981)

Mitchison, Rosalind, *A History of Scotland* (Methuen & Co., 1970)

Prebble, John, *The Lion in the North* (Secker & Warburg Ltd, 1971)

Detailed background reading:

Baynes, John, *The Jacobite Rising of 1715* (Cassell, 1970)

Buchan, John, *Montrose* (James Thin, Edinburgh, 1979)

Cowan, Edward J., *Montrose: For Covenant and King* (Weidenfeld & Nicolson, 1977)

Drummond, Humphrey, *Our Man in Scotland: Sir Ralph Sadleir 1507–1587* (Leslie Frewin, 1969)

Gaunt, Peter, *The Cromwellian Gazeteer: An Illustrated Guide to Britain in the Civil War and Commonwealth* (Sutton Publishing Ltd, 1987)

Holt, Michael, *The Forty-Five: the last Jacobite Rebellion* (HMSO, Edinburgh, 1995)

Fisher, Andrew, *William Wallace* (John Donald, Edinburgh, 1986)

Gardiner, S.R., *History of the Great Civil War: Vol 3 1645–47* (Windrush, 1987)

Gardiner, S.R., *History of the Commonwealth & Protectorate: Vol 1 1649–50* (Windrush, 1988)

Lenman, Bruce, *The Jacobite Risings in Britain 1689–1746* (Eyre Methuen, 1980)

Linklater, Magnus and Hesketh, Lady Christian, *For King & Conscience: John Graham of Claverhouse, Viscount Dundee* (Weidenfeld & Nicolson, 1989)

Maclean, Fitzroy, *Bonnie Prince Charlie* (Weidenfeld & Nicolson, 1988)

MacNair Scott, Ronald, *Robert the Bruce, King of Scots* (Hutchinson, 1982)

Petrie, Sir Charles, *The Jacobite Movement – the last phase 1746–1807* (Eyre & Spottiswoode, 1950)

Prebble, John, *The Darien Disaster* (Secker & Warburg, 1968)
Scott, Andrew Murray, *Bonnie Dundee* (John Donald, Edinburgh, 1989)
Sinclair-Stevenson, Christopher, *Inglorious Rebellion: the Jacobite Risings of 1708, 1715 and 1719* (Hamish Hamilton Ltd, 1971)
Wedgwood, C.V., *Montrose* (Collins, 1952)
Whyte, Ian and Kathleen, *On the Trail of the Jacobites*, (Routledge, 1990)

Accounts of specific battles discussed in the text:
Black, Jeremy, *Culloden and the '45* (Sutton Publishing Ltd, 1993)
Hook, Michael and Ross, Walter, *The Forty-Five* (HMSO, Edinburgh, 1995)
Mackenzie, W.M., *The Battle of Bannockburn* (The Strong Oak Press Ltd, Stevenage, 1989)
Prebble, John, *Culloden* (Secker & Warburg, 1961)
Reid, Stuart, *The Battle of Kilsyth, 1645* (Partizan Press, Leigh on Sea, 1989)
Sked, Phil, *Culloden* (The National Trust for Scotland, Edinburgh, 1995)
Taylor, Colonel Cameron, *Bannockburn* (The National Trust for Scotland, Edinburgh, 1991)
Tomasson, Katherine and Buist, Francis, *Battles of the '45* (B.T. Batsford Ltd, 1962)
The Killiecrankie Story (The National Trust for Scotland, 1991)
Museum of Flight (National Museums of Scotland)
Woosnam-Savage, Robert, *1745: Charles Edward Stuart and the Jacobites* (HMSO, Edinburgh, 1995)

General accounts of Scottish battles:
Bennett, Martyn, *Traveller's Guide to the Battlefields of the English Civil War* (Ian Allan Ltd, 1986)
Fairbairn, Neil, *A Traveller's Guide to the Battlefields of Britain* (Evans Brothers, 1983)
Forbes, George, *Scottish Battles* (Lang Syne Publishers Ltd, Glasgow, 1996)
Green, Lt. Col. Howard, *Guide to the Battlefields of Britain & Ireland* (Constable & Co., 1973)
Guest, Ken and Denise, *British Battles* (Harper Collins, 1996)
Kinross, John, *Discovering Battlefields in Scotland* (Shire Publications, Princes Risborough, 1976)
Kinross, John, *The Battlefields of Britain* (David & Charles, Newton Abbot, 1979)
Marren, Peter, *Grampian Battlefields* (The Mercat Press, Edinburgh, 1993)
Rogers, Colonel H.C.B., *Battles and Generals of the Civil Wars 1642–1651* (Seeley Service & Co. Ltd, 1968)

Seymour, William, *Battles in Britain 1066–1547* (Sidgwick & Jackson, 1975)
Seymour, William, *Battles in Britain 1642–1746* (Sidgwick & Jackson, 1975)
Smith, David J., *Action Stations: Military Airfields of Scotland, the North-East and Northern Ireland* (Patrick Stephens Ltd, Cambridge, 1983)
Smurthwaite, David, *The Complete Guide to the Battlefields of Britain* (Michael Joseph Ltd, 1993)
Warner, Philip, *Famous Scottish Battles* (Leo Cooper, 1995)
Young, Peter and Adair, John, *From Hastings to Culloden* (Roundwood Press, Kineton, 1979)

General guides to the regions covered by this volume:
Morton, H.V., *In Search of Scotland* (Methuen & Co. Ltd, 1984)
Morton, H.V., *In Scotland Again* (Methuen & Co. Ltd, 1985)
Tomes, John, *Blue Guide to Scotland* (A & C Black, 1992)
Tranter, Nigel, *The Queen's Scotland: The Heartland* (Hodder & Stoughton, 1971)
Tranter, Nigel, *The Queen's Scotland: The North East* (Hodder & Stoughton, 1974)
Whyte, Ian & Kathleen, *Discovering East Lothian* (John Donald, Edinburgh, 1988)

Recommended Fiction:
Scott, Sir Walter, *A Legend of Montrose* (Macmillan, 1901)
Tranter, Nigel, *The Bruce Trilogy* (Coronet, Sevenoaks, 1985)
Tranter, Nigel, *The Wallace* (Hodder & Stoughton, 1980)
Tranter, Nigel, *Rough Wooing* (Hodder & Stoughton, 1986)
Tranter, Nigel, *Montrose: The Captain-General* (Hodder & Stoughton, 1973)

For an excellent all-round introduction to walking and rambling, see:
Westacott, H.D., *The Walker's Handbook* (Oxford Illustrated Press, Yeovil, 1980)

INDEX OF PERSONS

INDEX OF PLACES